2007 SUPPLEMENT

CASES AND MATERIALS

CONFLICT OF LAWS

TWELFTH EDITION

by

PETER HAY
L.Q.C. Lamar Professor of Law
Emory University
and
University Professor Emeritus
Technische Universität Dresden

RUSSELL J. WEINTRAUB
Professor of Law
Ben H. & Kitty King Powell Chair Emeritus
University of Texas School of Law

PATRICK J. BORCHERS
Dean and Professor of Law
Creighton University

FOUNDATION PRESS

2007

THOMSON
WEST

© 2006 FOUNDATION PRESS
© 2007 By FOUNDATION PRESS
      395 Hudson Street
      New York, NY 10014
      Phone Toll Free 1–877–888–1330
      Fax (212) 367–6799
      foundation–press.com
Printed in the United States of America

ISBN 978–1–59941–293–1

 TEXT IS PRINTED ON 10% POST CONSUMER RECYCLED PAPER

TABLE OF CONTENTS

*

TABLE OF CASES

Principal cases are in bold type. Non-principal cases are in roman type. References are to Pages.

vii

2007 SUPPLEMENT

CASES AND MATERIALS

CONFLICT OF LAWS

*

CHAPTER 2

DOMICILE: THE CHOSEN POINT OF ENTRY

5. SPECIAL SITUATIONS

Page 29, insert in Note 1:

Gaudin v. Remis, 379 F.3d 631 (9th Cir. 2004). Father removed two children from Canada to Hawaii. Mother, a Canadian citizen, traveled to Hawaii as a "nonimmigrant alien" and filed a petition to have the children returned to Canada pursuant to the Hague Convention on the Civil Aspects of International Child Abduction. The court had previously ruled that the petition was moot if the mother had moved permanently to Hawaii. Now the court noted that the statutory definition of "nonimmigrant alien" is a person who has no intention of abandoning the alien's residence in a foreign country. Applying "the federal common law of domicile" the court held that the mother "is barred by law from possessing the requisite intent to establish domicile in Hawaii. Because she cannot lawfully have moved permanently to Hawaii, the case is not moot, and the [district] court erred in so holding." Id. at 638.

Mark v. Mark, [2005] 3 All E.R. 912 (H.L. 2005). A Nigerian national began divorce proceedings in England. At that time she had overstayed her visa and her presence in England was unlawful. The husband contested the English court's jurisdiction on the ground that the wife did not have the requisite domicile in England. Baroness Hale of Richmond wrote the opinion for the House of Lords upholding jurisdiction to divorce: "[T]here is no reason in principle why a person whose presence here is unlawful cannot acquire a domicile of choice in this country. Although her presence here is a criminal offence, it is by no means clear that she will be required to leave if the position is discovered." Id. at 930.

CHAPTER 3

JURISDICTION OF COURTS

SECTION 2. BASES OF JUDICIAL JURISDICTION OVER NATURAL AND LEGAL PERSONS

B. IN SEARCH OF NEW JURISDICTIONAL STANDARDS: THE ERA OF INTERNATIONAL SHOE, "MINIMUM CONTACTS", AND "FAIRNESS"

Page 78, insert in Note 3:

Tedford v. Warner–Lambert Co., 327 F.3d 423 (5th Cir. 2003), resolved as a matter of first impression the relationship between the one-year removal limit of 28 U.S.C. § 1446(b) and the "voluntary act by the plaintiff" basis for removal. Plaintiff brought a products liability suit against a pharmaceutical manufacturer in a Texas state court. She joined as a defendant a Texas doctor, thus preventing removal to federal court. Plaintiff signed a nonsuit of the doctor before the one-year anniversary of the commencement of her action, but did not notify the pharmaceutical manufacturer of the nonsuit until the year had expired. Held: The defendant could remove to federal court. "Where a plaintiff has attempted to manipulate the statutory rules for determining federal removal jurisdiction, thereby preventing the defendant from exercising its rights, equity may require that the one-year limit in § 1446(b) be extended. The facts of this case present just such a circumstance." Id. at 428–29.

Page 83, add to the end of Note 4:

A variant of this question arose in Yahoo! Inc. v. La Ligue Contre Le Racisme, 433 F.3d 1199 (9th Cir. 2006) (en banc). In that case, the plaintiff was a California-based provider of various Internet-related products, including an auction site. The defendant, a French entity, brought suit in the French courts to prevent the plaintiff from allowing the sale of Nazi memorabilia to French buyers, because to do so would violate various French laws. The defendant was successful in obtaining various orders from a French court that purported to impose substantial monetary penalties on Yahoo!. Yahoo! then brought a diversity action in a California federal court against the French entity for a declaration that the French decrees were unenforceable against it. A majority of the en banc judges Ninth Circuit ruled that there was personal jurisdiction because the decrees were aimed a Yahoo! and caused it significant harm in California.

In so doing, the Ninth Circuit reasoned from *Keeton* as follows:

We take this opportunity to clarify our law and to state that the "brunt" of the harm need not be suffered in the forum state. If a jurisdictionally sufficient amount of harm is suffered in the forum state, it does not matter that even more harm might have been suffered in another state. In so stating we are following *Keeton*, decided the same day as *Calder*, in which the Court sustained the exercise of personal jurisdiction in New Hampshire even though "it is undoubtedly true that the bulk of the harm done to petitioner occurred outside New Hampshire."

Should the fraction of the harm felt by the plaintiff in the forum be of constitutional significance? For discussion of other aspects of the *Yahoo!* litigation see infra Casebook p. 323. Although a majority of the judges upheld personal jurisdiction over the French defendants, the three judges who ruled that there was no jurisdiction combined with three judges who held that the case was not ripe for decision. The bare majority of six judges remanded the case with the direction to dismiss without prejudice. See infra Casebook p. 323.

Page 99, add to the end of Note 1:

An interesting example of a product meeting the "special design" factor that Justice O'Connor identified as showing a purposeful connection with the forum state's market occurred in Paz v. Brush Engineered Materials, Inc., 445 F.3d 809 (5th Cir. 2006). In that case, a California defendant manufactured parts for the space shuttle assembled in the forum state of Mississippi. The parts were alleged to create dangerous airborne levels of a radioactive substance. The court found the stream of commerce test met because the only possible use of these products was in the assembly of the shuttles in Mississippi.

Page 100, Note 6, add at very end of the page:

The proposed Chinese rule for jurisdiction in products liability cases is the same: Chinese courts have jurisdiction if injury was suffered in China or the product was manufactured or sold there. Art. 37, Model Law of Private International Law, Peoples' Republic of China (6th, and current, draft 2000). In the European Community, Art. 15(1)(c) of the Brussels–I Regulation, infra Casebook p. 1008, would also support jurisdiction on similar facts.

Page 108, insert in Note 2:

See Spenser, Jurisdiction and the Internet: Returning to Traditional Principles to Analyze Network–Mediated Contacts, 2006 U. Ill. L. Rev. 71, 100: "Prevailing approaches to evaluating assertion of jurisdiction based on Internet activity frustrate *Calder*'s proper application where an intentional tort is at issue because they focus on the target for Web content rather than the target of wrongdoing—the alleged victim in the case."

Page 109, add to the end of Note 2:

See also Fenn v. Mleads Enterprises, Inc., 137 P.3d 706 (Utah 2006) (out-of-state company that sent an unsolicited email to a plaintiff without knowing the plaintiff's physical location not subject to jurisdiction in the plaintiff's home state in a claim arising out of the email).

Page 109, add to the end of Note 4:

Can the principal case be squared with the California Supreme Court's later opinion in Snowney v. Harrah's Entertainment, Inc., 112 P.3d 28 (Cal. 2005)? In that case, a California consumer booked a stay in a Nevada hotel that accepted reservations over its Internet site and also advertised in California in other ways. The consumer alleged that the hotel misrepresented the terms of his room rate by failing to disclose a three-dollar-per-night energy surcharge. The hotel objected to the California court's assertion of personal jurisdiction but the California Supreme Court held that specific jurisdiction was established by the purposeful activities of the hotel in attracting California patrons.

A related issue that often arises in these fact patterns is the degree to which the activities of domestic subsidiaries can be attributed to foreign corporations. For example, in Stubbs v. Wyndham Nassau Resort, 447 F.3d 1357 (11th Cir. 2006), the plaintiff was injured at a Bahamian resort but brought suit in Florida. The circuit court ruled that the Florida subsidiaries of the Bahamian corporate owner "conducted business solely for the nonresident corporation . . . and thus their activities could be imputed to the nonresident corporations." Id. at 1362. In light of the material supra Casebook pp. 84–85 in Note 6 should conducting business "solely" for a nonresident defendant be sufficient to impute the activities of a local subsidiary to the nonresident? What sort of information would you gather in discovery to attempt to prove or disprove a sufficient connection to meet this standard?

Page 111, add to the text at the end of the Note on Special Problems of Personal Jurisdiction in the Federal Courts:

An interesting use of FRCP 4(k)(2) occurred in Odilla Mutaka Mwani v. Osama Bin Laden, 417 F.3d 1 (D.C. Cir. 2005), in which the court concluded that bin Laden's aggregate contacts with the U.S. were sufficient to establish personal jurisdiction over him on claims by various Kenyan victims who were injured in the notorious bombing of the U.S. embassy there.

Page 120, add to the end of Note 4:

Tuazon v. R.J. Reynolds Tobacco Co., 433 F.3d 1163 (9th Cir. 2006) (tobacco company's extensive advertising and sales in the forum state give rise to general jurisdiction).

SECTION 3.   JURISDICTION OVER "THINGS"

Page 142, add to Note 4 at the end:

In the European Community, the European Court of Justice has held that protective orders and decisions that issue ex parte are not entitled to recognition in another member state. ECR 1980, 1553 (*Denilauer*). Even when a "freezing injunction" (*Mareva* injunction) issues after judgment, i.e. is intended to facilitate enforcement and execution, it seems incompatible with Art. 22 No. 5 of the Brussels–I Regulation which establishes the exclusive jurisdiction of the courts of the recognizing Member State. Nevertheless, Switzerland—under the parallel provision of the Lugano Convention—(BGE vol.129, III, 226 (2003)) and France (Cour de Cassation, 1re civ., June 30, 2004, reported and criticized by Schlosser, [2006] IPRax 300), have extended recognition, the latter court on the ground that the right to a hearing was not impaired because the respondent could have sought modification or setting aside of the order. As Schlosser, supra, notes, this view renders the "right to be heard" that underlies the *Denilauer* decision all but meaningless.

Page 142, add to Note 5:

The proposed Chinese law would expressly provide for jurisdiction under these circumstances: Art. 52 of the Model Law, supra Casebook p. 100, Note 6, this Supplement p. 3.

SECTION 4.   COMPETENCE OF COURT AND NOTICE

Page 155, add to Note 2:

In Jones v. Flowers, 547 U.S. 220 (2006), the U.S. Supreme Court held that registered mail sent to a taxpayer at the property's address was insufficient notice for a tax sale of an $80,000 home where the letters had twice been returned undeliverable. The majority analogized the failure to follow up on the returned letters to seeing "the departing postman accidentally drop[] the letters down the storm drain." Id. at 1716. Would follow-up measures be required if it were a matter of a $25 parking ticket rather than valuable real estate? For a suggestion that the constitutional standard would be less demanding in the case of a $25 parking ticket, see Patrick J. Borchers, Jones v. Flowers: An Essay on a Unified Theory of Procedural Due Process, 40 Creighton L. Rev. ___ (2007).

CHAPTER 4

LIMITATIONS ON THE EXERCISE OF JURISDICTION

SECTION 1.   LIMITATIONS IMPOSED BY CONTRACT

Page 168, insert a new Note 4:

4. In extension of the policy expressed in *Scherk*, *Mitsubishi*, Casebook p. 167, Note 1, and other cases, federal courts have applied *M/S Bremen* to uphold choice of forum clauses in cases (e.g., involving personal injuries) arising out of contracts of maritime employment. See, e.g., Marinechance Shipping, Ltd. v. Sebastian, 143 F.3d 216 (5th Cir. 1998), cert. denied, 525 U.S. 1055, 119 S.Ct. 620 (1998); Francisco v. M/T Stolt Achievement, 293 F.3d 270 (5th Cir. 2002), cert. denied, 537 U.S. 1030 (2002); Bautista v. Star Cruises, 396 F.3d 1289 (11th Cir. 2005); Lim v. Offshore Specialty Fabricators, Inc., 404 F.3d 898 (5th Cir. 2005), cert. denied, ___ U.S. ___, 126 S.Ct. 365 (2005).

Page 170, insert in Note 1:

Casavant v. Norwegian Cruise Line, Ltd., 829 N.E.2d 1171 (Mass. App. 2005), rev. denied, 834 N.E.2d 256 (Mass. 2005), cert. denied, 126 S.Ct. 1337 (2006), refused to enforce a forum-selection clause in a cruise contract. The court held that the clause was not binding because the defendant did not deliver the contract to the plaintiffs until almost a year after the original booking and two months after full payment of the cruise price. The court summarized the view that federal courts have taken of the enforceability of forum clauses:

> In the wake of *Carnival Cruise*, the Federal courts have decided a number of cases which establish that, for vacation cruise ticketing contracts, in order for the passenger to be bound by the forum selection clause under Federal maritime law, the private ticket cruise buyer must be given reasonable time within which to act and to reject the ticketing contract and forum selection clause, without incurring disproportionately unfair penalties for such a rejection.

Id. at 1180.

Page 171, Note 2, add at the end:

What claims are governed by a particular forum selection clause? "Usually courts have given clauses a transactional reading, meaning that all claims that are part of the same transaction are covered by the clause." E. Scoles, P. Hay, P. Borchers, S. Symeonides, Conflict of Laws § 11.6 at 490 (4th ed. 2004), with references. In Quebecor World (USA), Inc. v. Harsha Associates, L.L.C., 455 F.Supp.2d 236, 238–39 (W.D.N.Y. 2006), the court held that a forum selection in a guaranty did not carry over to the underlying contract because the two were not closely enough related. "Relevant factors include whether the two documents were executed contemporaneously, whether the guaranty is stated to have been an inducement or consideration for the contract or incorporates the contract by reference, and whether the two documents cover the identical subject matter."

Page 172, insert in Note 4:

In Idaho, one of the three states that do not enforce choice-of-forum agreements, courts base this refusal on Idaho Code § 29–110(1), which provides: "Every stipulation or condition in a contract, by which any party thereto is restricted from enforcing his rights under the contract by the usual proceedings in the ordinary tribunals, or which limits the time within which he may thus enforce his rights, is void." In Fisk v. Royal Caribbean Cruises, Ltd., 108 P.3d 990 (Id. 2005), however, the court enforced a forum agreement in a cruise contract holding that federal maritime law, as set out in Carnival Cruise, supra Casebook p. 168, preempted Idaho law.

Page 173, insert a new Note 4a:

4a. Absent federal-state or public policy concerns, what law governs the interpretation of a forum selection clause (see also supra)? For the view that it is the law chosen by the parties, see Yavuz v. 61 MM, Ltd., 465 F.3d 418, 427–428 (10th Cir. 2006), concluding that Swiss law, which the parties chose, determines whether the forum-selection clause is mandatory or permissive and what parties and issues the clause covers. The clause is part of the contract and should be governed by the law applicable by it. European law tends to view the contract, the choice-of-forum, and the choice-of-law agreements as—at least conceptually—separate contracts so that, occasionally, one might be valid under its applicable law, while another might not be.

Page 174, Note 9, add to first paragraph:

What if the parties chose the court of a third (non-EU) state but the defendant has his/her domicile or principal place of domicile in the EU: may the defendant be sued at his/her domicile or principal place of business (Art.2 or 60, respectively, Brussels–I Regulation) or must the suit be dismissed under Art. 23? A (declaratory) Opinion of the EC Court of Justice concludes that the answer is "yes, the action may be maintained:" the exclusivity character of Art. 23 works only in favor of an EU forum chosen by the parties; the choice of a third-country forum, however, is trumped by the Regulation's jurisdictional provisions defining the jurisdiction of courts within the EU. The question arose in the context of the renewal of the "Lugano (Parallel) Convention," infra Casebook p. 1002: Switzerland, for instance, will be treated the same as an EU member and a choice of its courts will be exclusive; if, in contrast, third-country treatment applied, jurisdiction would lie, in contravention of a stipulation in favor of Switzerland, at the French domicile/place of business of the defendant. Opinion 1/03, [2006] ECR I–01145 (Competence of the Community to Conclude the New Lugano Convention . . .), ¶ 153 et seq. See Anno., 13 Colum. J. Eur. L. 189, 195–96 (2006/2007).

In 2005, the Hague Conference on Private International Law proposed a Convention on Choice of Court Agreements which is designed to parallel the New York Convention on the Recognition and Enforcement of Foreign Arbitral Awards. It would apply to exclusive forum selection agreements and, if widely adopted, will provide "business parties . . . [with] an alternative to choosing arbitration in their contracts." If the EC were to become a party, the Convention would apply between it and a contracting state and the resulting effect of an exclusive forum selection clause in favor of an EC (or Lugano) state would be the same as described in the preceding paragraph. Kruger, The 20th Session of the Hague Conference: A New Choice of Court Convention and the Issue of EC Membership, 55 Int. & Comp. L.Q. 447 (2006).

For criticism of the non-exclusive treatment given forum selection clauses in favor of a third country and for discussion of the availability of damages (under English law) for breach of such a forum selection clause, see L. Merrett, The Enforcement of Jurisdiction Agreements Within the Brussels Regime, 55 Int'l & Comp.L. Q. 315 (2006).

SECTION 2.   FRAUD, FORCE AND PRIVILEGE

Page 177, insert at end of Note 5:

The Antiterrorist and Effective Death Penalty Act of 1996 (AEDPA), 18 U.S.C. § 32 (1996), among other things, amended the Foreign Sovereign Immunities Act, eliminating immunity for countries designated as supporters of terrorism. When there is a claim based, for instance, on the Torture Victim Protection Act of 1992 (28 U.S.C. § 1350, Note) or the Alien Torts Statute (id.), the AEDPA provides for adjudicatory jurisdiction. See, e.g., Salazar v. Islamic Republic of Iran, 370 F.Supp.2d 105 (D.D.C. 2005).

SECTION 3.   FORUM NON CONVENIENS

Page 182, insert in Note 1:

Sinochem Int'l Co. v. Malaysia Int'l Shipping, 127 S.Ct. 1184 (2007), resolved a conflict among Circuits as to whether a district court can grant a defendant's motion for a forum non conveniens dismissal without first determining that it has subject matter jurisdiction and personal jurisdiction over the defendant. A Malaysian company sued a Chinese company for damages resulting from the Chinese company's alleged misrepresentations to a Chinese court. The opinion states that "where [as in this case] subject-matter or personal jurisdiction is difficult to determine, and *forum non conveniens* considerations weigh heavily in favor of dismissal, the court properly takes the less burdensome course."

Page 190, top, add a new second paragraph to Note 6:

Texas law permits a dismissal or stay for forum non conveniens when the plaintiff is a non-resident but forbids it when the plaintiff is a "legal resident" of Texas. Tex. Civ. Prac. & Rem. Code Ann. § 71.05(e) (1997). Does this provision violate obligations undertaken by the United States in many bilateral treaties of Friendship, Commerce, and Navigation to afford citizens of the other treaty party national treatment with respect to access to courts? Does it violate U.S. obligations as a signatory of the International Covenant on Civil and Political Rights, which forbids discrimination against "all individuals within its territory" on the grounds of "race, colour, sex, language, religion, political or other opinion, national or social origin, property, birth or other status." The question has been the subject of debate between Professor Weintraub (= no violation) and Professor Paust (= violation): Weintraub, International Litigation and Forum Non Conveniens, 29 Tex. Int'l L.J. 321, 349 (1994); Paust, "Equal Treaty Rights," Resident Status and Forum Non Conveniens, 26 Hou. J. Int'l L. 405, 409 (2004); Weintraub, "Equal Treaty Rights": A Response to Professor Paust, 27 id. 241 (2005); Paust, Discrimination on the Basis of Resident Status and Denial of Equal Treatment: A Reply to Professor Weintraub's Response, id. at 253 (2005).

Page 190, insert, Note 7, at the end:

For *Hong Kong* and some comparative treatment, see Svantesson, In Defence of the Doctrine for Forum Non Conveniens, 35 Hong Kong L.J. 395 (2005).

Page 191, insert as a new paragraph to Note 8:

In re Harrods has been dealt a mortal blow. In Case C–281/02, Owusu v. Jackson, [2005] ECR 1–1383, [2005] 1 Lloyd's Rep. 452, [2005] 2 W.L.R. 942, the Court of Justice of the European Communities held that an English court could not grant a forum non conveniens stay of a suit brought by an English domiciliary against an English company and several Jamaican defendants to recovery for injuries suffered while the plaintiff was diving in the sea during a vacation in Jamaica. The Court ruled that the Brussels Convention precludes an EU court "from declining the jurisdiction conferred on it by Article 2 of that convention [now Article 2 of the Regulation] on the ground that a court of a non-Contracting State would be a more appropriate forum for the trial of the action even if the jurisdiction of no other Contracting State is in issue or the proceedings have no connecting factors to any other Contracting State."

Outside the Common Law and Western European contexts, the forum-non-conveniens doctrine has been proposed for adoption in China. Art. 51 of the Model Law on Private International Law of the People's Republic of China (6th draft, 2000) expressly provides for application of the doctrine and does so on conditions essentially similar to American law. The Supreme Court of Japan has developed a doctrine similar to forum non conveniens. In Family Co. Ltd. v. Miyahara, [1998] H.J. (1626) 74, translation in Japanese Annual Int'l L. 117 (1998), the Supreme Court of Japan held that Japanese courts did not have jurisdiction of a Japanese company's suit to recover funds from an individual residing in Frankfurt. The company had given the Frankfurt resident the funds to purchase goods for the company. The court held that in international cases jurisdiction is based on rules of reason for maintaining impartiality, fairness, and speediness. The court then stated: "However, if we find some exceptional circumstances, where a trial in a Japanese court would result in contradicting the ideas of promoting fairness between the parties and equitable and prompt administration of justice, the international adjudicatory jurisdiction of the Japanese court should be denied." The court found such exceptional circumstances in this case. The contract between the parties was made in Germany, defendant had his home and principal place of business in Germany for more than 20 years, and much of the evidence relevant to the defense is in Germany.

CHAPTER 5

FOREIGN JUDGMENTS

SECTION 1. POLICIES UNDERLYING THE RECOGNITION AND ENFORCEMENT OF FOREIGN JUDGMENTS

Page 220, Note 4, at the end of the second paragraph, add:

After the preliminary injunction in *Bertelsmann* had been extended three times but the petition had never been decided on the merits, Bertelsmann withdrew its complaint [see 2005 RIW No. 2, p. II] and the Bundesverfassungsgericht then lifted the preliminary injunction: Decision of November 9, 2005, 2 BvR 1198/03. The constitutional question therefore still remains unresolved. For detailed analysis, see Rasmussen–Bonne, Zum Stand der Rechtshilfepraxis bei Zustellungsersuchen von US–Schadensersatzklagen nach dem Beschluss des Bundesverfassungsgerichts vom 25. Juli 2003, in Rasmussen–Bonne, Freer, Lüke & Weitnauer (eds.), Balancing of Interests–Festschrift für Peter Hay 323 (2005).

Note 4, at the end, add:

With respect to the defense of lack of reciprocity, see infra Casebook p. 222 Note 8, new second and third paragraphs (this Supplement).

Page 222, Note 8, add new second and third paragraphs:

German law retains a reciprocity requirement for the recognition of non-EU country judgments. Code of Civil Procedure (ZPO) § 328(1) No. 5. In keeping with general German recognition practice (see supra No. 4), this requirement has been construed in a pro-recognition fashion. Thus, in a German–American recognition case, the German judgment debtor resisted recognition because the successful American claimants (plaintiffs in the original action, now judgment creditors) would recover their court and attorneys' costs of the enforcement proceeding under applicable German law, while German claimants in reverse cases in American courts bear their own costs. Since a German judgment creditor would thus recover less than the full value of his or her German judgment in the United States (i.e., judgment less costs and fees), so the argument went, reciprocity in judgment recognition is not assured with respect to the United States. This argument of course overlooks that the German creditor, having been awarded his or her costs in all antecedent German proceedings, may recover these in the United States as part of the judgment, while the reverse is not true. Without addressing the last point, the German Supreme Court pointed to an earlier decision, in which it had held that the " 'American rule of costs' violates neither basic rights of the parties nor general principles of the rule of law [due process]," and held that reciprocity with respect to the United States is assured, "at least in those cases in which the amount to be recognized and enforced [in Germany] ... exceeds the attorneys' fees [in the United States]." Bundesgerichtshof (BGH), Decision of October 20, 2005, SGL Acotec v.

American Ins. Co., Dock No. IX ZR 246/03, at No. 5; briefly noted by M. Stürner, jurisPR–BGHZivilR 51/2005, anno. 3.

In the United States, the American Law Institute adopted a proposal for a federal "Foreign Judgments and Enforcement Act" in 2005. The drafters noted that American courts had gone in different directions after *Hilton*, with most having adopted the dissenting view, and that it was desirable that "state as well as federal courts [be] held to a uniform national standard, thus both avoiding forum-shopping in enforcing foreign-country judgments and affording to foreign courts [for the reverse case] a clear picture of practice in the United States." ALI, Proposed Foreign Judgments Recognition and Enforcement Act (2005), § 7, comment *a*. These goals could be achieved either by adopting or by rejecting a reciprocity requirement as a matter of national law. The proposed act opts for the former: "A foreign judgment shall not be recognized or enforced in a court in the United States if the court finds that comparable judgments of courts of the United States would not be recognized or enforced in the courts of the state of origin." § 7(a). Subsection (e) contemplates agreements between the United States and foreign states, "setting forth reciprocal practices." By opting in favor of a reciprocity requirement, the proponents seek "to create an incentive to foreign countries to commit to recognition and enforcement of judgments rendered in the United States." § 7, comment *b*. The proposal thus favors a public interest goal over a private party's interest in the recognition and enforcement of a foreign judgment that is otherwise free of jurisdictional or procedural defects. For a different view of the appropriate respective roles of public and private interests, see—in the context of *forum non conveniens*—the House of Lords' decision in Lubbe v. Cape Plc, supra Casebook p. 183 and accompanying Notes. Further: In the absence of agreements, such as envisioned by subsection (e) of the proposed provision, will adoption of a reciprocity requirement by the United States be likely to contribute to pro-recognition practices on the part of foreign courts—such as in the case of the German Supreme Court's decision reported in the preceding paragraph—or invite a harder look at United States practice?A comprehensive historical review of the reciprocity requirement, which also addresses the ALI proposal, addresses the intersection of private and public international law and the question whether governments do or should have and promote a "public" interest in private litigation. It concludes that there is a public interest because of the transaction costs of non-recognition of judgments on international trade. "Individual actions can and do affect international relations and national interests. . . . With globalization, universal judgment recognition can only become more important, and judgments reciprocity is an effective means of promoting it." Note, Shaky Foundations: Criticism of Reciprocity and the Distinction Between Public and Private International Law, 38 N.Y.U. J. Int'l & L. Pol. 221, 279 (2006). Do you agree?

SECTION 2.   RECOGNITION AND ENFORCEMENT IN GENERAL

A.   IN PERSONAM JUDGMENTS

Page 230, insert as Note 4:

4. Just as a judgment registered under § 1963 becomes an F–2 judgment subject to F–2 rules, a judgment registered in a state under the Uniform Enforcement of

Foreign Judgments Act, below, may be treated as a local judgment. In National Bank of Arizona v. Moore, 122 P.3d 1265 (N.M. App. 2005), cert. denied, 122 P.3d 1263 (N.M. 2005), Bank recovered a judgment in Arizona against an Arizona husband. Arizona and New Mexico are both community property states. The judgment was for husband's separate debt, not a community debt. Bank registered the judgment in New Mexico under the Uniform Act. Under Arizona law but not New Mexico law a judgment for a spouse's separate debt cannot be enforced against community property. Held: the registered judgment may be enforced against a New Mexico bank account that is community property. "Once the Arizona judgment was converted into a New Mexico judgment, New Mexico law was applicable to the enforcement of that judgment." 122 P.2d at 1267. "To the extent Husband argues that the law applicable to the enforcement of the judgment against him depends on whether the bank account is Arizona community property as opposed to New Mexico community property, Husband did not make this argument below. We therefore decline to address this contention." Id. at 1268.

SECTION 3.   PARTICULAR EFFECTS

A.   PERSONS AFFECTED

Page 239, insert in Note 2:

State v. Homeside Lending, Inc., 826 A.2d 997 (Vt. 2003), held that Vermont members of a national class action in an Alabama state court are not bound by the judgment of that court approving a settlement because the Alabama proceeding violated their due process rights. Notice of the opportunity to opt out of the class action did not adequately inform members of the potential burdens of the litigation. The class representatives did not adequately represent absent class members because the incentive payments to the representatives provided an economic benefit far greater than the value of the settlement. Moreover, when a class action can impose monetary burdens on class members that exceed any benefits, a state court has personal jurisdiction only over those class members who have minimum contacts with the state.

Page 243, insert in Note 2:

Headwaters Inc. v. U.S. Forest Service, 399 F.3d 1047 (9th Cir. 2005). A non-profit environmental organization sued the U.S. Forest Service (USFS) alleging failure to comply with environmental laws when approving timber sales in national forests. The district court dismissed the lawsuit. Then Headwaters, another non-profit environmental organization, sued the USFS alleging the same failure to comply with environmental laws. The district court dismissed the action on the ground that plaintiff was precluded by the judgment in the prior action. Held: Reversed.

> The district court held, *sua sponte*, that two environmental organizations who have never litigated the validity of several timber sales are precluded from doing so because counsel for other organizations, a year earlier, signed a dismissal with prejudice of a similar suit. We have in this nation a " 'deep-rooted historic tradition that everyone should have his own day in court,' "and presume, consequently, that " '[a] judgment or decree among parties to a

lawsuit resolves issues as among them, but it does not conclude the rights of strangers to those proceedings.' "*Richards v. Jefferson County*, 517 U.S. 793, 798, 116 S.Ct. 1761, 135 L.Ed.2d 76 (1996) (quoting *Martin v. Wilks*, 490 U.S. 755, 762, 109 S.Ct. 2180, 104 L.Ed.2d 835 (1989)). While there are narrow exceptions to this principle, usually denominated by the term "privity," the district court here applied the privity doctrine without establishing, among other prerequisites, that the present plaintiffs were adequately represented in the prior suit, and without giving plaintiffs an opportunity to demonstrate that they were not. We reverse, and remand for consideration of the preclusion question after full adversary airing and a development of an appropriate record.

Id. at 1050.

B.   ISSUES AFFECTED

Page 250, insert before last paragraph:

    See also National Bank of Arizona v. Moore, 122 P.3d 1265 (N.M.App. 2005), enforcing an Arizona judgment against the debtor's separate (non-community property) debt against his New Mexico community property, noted at supra Casebook p. 230 Note 4, supra this Supplement. While the judgment could not have been enforced against Arizona community property, the court concluded that New Mexico's wider enforcement standard applied and that the Full Faith and Credit Clause did not prevent the enforcing court from giving a judgment "greater force" than it has where rendered. 122 P.3d at 1269. The problem is the same, but the conflict perhaps more exacerbated, when the local (enforcing) state's policy is the result of an earlier inconsistent judgment. See Colby v. Colby, infra Casebook p. 297, note 4. Does the Supreme Court's decision in *Treinies*, infra Casebook p. 295, speak to either or both of these problems, either as matter of law (*Colby*) or of policy (*Moore* and *Hart*)?

C.   LIMITATIONS ON FULL FAITH AND CREDIT

Page 264, insert as Note 5:

5.   In the principal case Justice Ginsburg states that "[e]nforcement measures do not travel with the sister state judgment." But cf. 18 U.S.C. § 2265(a), requiring that sister-state protection orders against domestic violence and stalking "shall be accorded full faith and credit by the court of another State . . . and enforced as if it were the order of the enforcing State."

SECTION 4.   DEFENSES

B.   NATURE OF ORIGINAL CAUSE OF ACTION

Page 315, add a new paragraph to Note 2:

    Concern has been raised that the strict recognition command of Community law may preclude the kind of review that would assure compliance with Art. 6 of the European Human Rights Convention's guarantee of a fair trial. The EC Court's decision in *Denilauler*, supra Casebook p. 288, Note (1), addresses this concern in part when it restricts the recognition command to judgments that issue in adversary proceedings. However, violations of Art. 6 might also occur in such a proceeding. It has therefore been suggested that the public policy exception should be used more extensively to assure compliance with Art. 6, "providing that there is some tightening up of when the defence would operate." J. Fawcett, The Impact of Art. 6 of the ECHR on Private International Law, 56 Int'l & Comp. L.Q. 1, 44 (2007).

D.   FOREIGN COUNTRY JUDGMENTS

Page 323, insert in Note 2:

Yahoo! Inc. v. La Ligue Contre Le Racisme et L'Antisemitisme, 379 F.3d 1120 (9th Cir. 2004), by a 2–1 panel vote, reversed the district court on the ground that there was no personal jurisdiction over the French defendants. On rehearing en banc, 433 F.3d 1199 (9th Cir. en banc 2006), a majority of 8 judges concluded that the district court had personal jurisdiction over the defendants. Of that majority, 3 judges concluded that the action should be dismissed for lack or ripeness: "[I]t is extremely unlikely that any penalty, if assessed, could ever be enforced against Yahoo! in the United States. Further, First Amendment harm may not exist at all, given the possibility that Yahoo! has now 'in large measure' complied with the French court's orders. . . . There is some possibility that in further restricting access to [Internet users located in France] Yahoo! might have to restrict access by American users. But this possibility is, at this point, highly speculative."

Three judges held that the case is ripe for adjudication but "that the District Court did not properly exercise personal jurisdiction over the defendants and also should have abstained under the Act of State Doctrine (see Banco Nacional de Cuba v. Sabbatino, Casebook p. 719) from deciding Yahoo!'s claims." When the 3 votes that the suit is unripe are combined with the 3 votes that there is no personal jurisdiction over the defendants, there is a bare majority (6–5) to dismiss. Therefore the Ninth Circuit en banc reversed the district court opinion and remanded with instructions to dismiss without prejudice.

Five judges held that the case was ripe for adjudication, that there was personal jurisdiction over the defendants, and would remand for further briefing and factfinding on the issue of whether "Yahoo! is not harmed by the very threat of the French orders' possible enforcement."

Page 324, insert as Note 5:

5. In Saldanha v. Beals, [2003] 3 S.C.R. 416, the Supreme Court of Canada required an Ontario court to enforce a Florida default judgment against Ontario residents including both treble and punitive damages. The majority held that the Ontario court must enforce the judgment even if it will bankrupt the defendants. The basis for liability was the sale of Florida land to a developer for $8,000. With interest the judgment is over $1 million Canadian. Morguard Investments v. De Savoye, [1990] 3 S.C.R. 1077, required full faith and credit to judgments of another Canadian province. *Saldanha* extends *Morguard* to judgments of foreign countries subject to defenses such as those in § 4 of the Uniform Foreign Money–Judgments Recognition Act. See Casebook p. 320. Two dissenters agree that Canadian courts should enforce foreign judgments but balk under the circumstances of this case. One dissenter would impose greater barriers to enforcement of foreign judgments than the majority indicates.

The decision not to defend the Florida action was based on advice by an Ontario solicitor that a Canadian court would not enforce the Florida judgment because the Florida court would not have jurisdiction over the defendants unless they appeared. The defendants were not aware of the risk of a large judgment because, as in many states, Florida courts require pleading only that the amount in controversy is in excess of the stated jurisdictional amount. The solicitor's malpractice insurer paid the judgment.

CHAPTER 6

THE IMPACT OF THE CONSTITUTION

SECTION 2. CHOICE OF LAW

B. MODERN APPROACH

Page 360, insert as Note 3:

3. VantagePoint Venture Partners v. Examen, Inc., 871 A.2d 1108 (Del. 2005). The merger of two Delaware corporations was imminent. A preferred shareholder of one of the corporations claimed that the corporation was a "quasi-California corporation" under the California Corporation Code because more than 50% of its property, payroll payments, sales, and stockholders were in California. As a quasi-California corporation the shareholder claimed that that the corporation was governed by California law under which, unlike Delaware law, preferred shareholders were entitled to vote as a separate class on the merger. The Delaware Supreme Court held that Delaware law controlled and that the Due Process and Commerce Clauses of the U.S. Constitution mandated this result. Contrary to Justice Brennan's statement in footnote 10 of the principal case, is the result compelled by the Full Faith and Credit Clause because this is a rare instance in which there is a compelling national need for a uniform answer under the law of the state of incorporation?

Page 376, insert in Note 2:

Boyd v. Goffoli, 608 S.E.2d 169 (W.Va. 2004). Plaintiffs applied to defendant trucking company in West Virginia for training as truck drivers and for employment. Defendant falsely told plaintiffs that they could obtain commercial driver's licenses in a course in Pennsylvania and transfer these licenses back to West Virginia. When plaintiffs were denied licenses they sued defendant and were each awarded $75,000 compensatory damages and $250,000 punitive damages. Defendant appealed claiming "that it was improperly punished for a scheme to violate Pennsylvania law in contravention of *State Farm Mut. Auto. Ins. Co. v. Campbell.*" Held: affirmed:

> Reading the Supreme Court's pronouncements in *Campbell* and *Shutts* together, this Court now holds that a State has a legitimate interest in imposing damages to punish a defendant for unlawful acts committed outside of the State's jurisdiction where the State has a significant contact or significant aggregation of contacts to the plaintiffs' claims which arise from the unlawful out-of-state conduct. We now apply this rule to the instant facts.

> First, we note that the facts in *Shutts* are quite different from those below. In *Shutts*, Kansas law was applied to all of the claims despite the fact that the vast majority of those claims had no connection to Kansas. In contrast, Appellees were all West Virginia residents who were initially informed of the

Pennsylvania scheme, and wrongly assured that it was legal by Appellant's agent who was a resident of West Virginia. Further, Appellees' economic losses occurred in West Virginia. Therefore, West Virginia has a significant contact with the claims asserted by Appellees. As a result, the fact that a portion of Appellant's misconduct occurred in Pennsylvania is legally insignificant. Certainly, a West Virginia court has an interest in protecting its citizens from tortious conduct and is not precluded from doing so simply because some of the tortious conduct occurred in another state.

Id. at 179.

CHAPTER 7

THRESHOLD PROBLEMS OF THE FORUM IN CHOICE OF LAW

SECTION 1. ADMITTING OR REJECTING THE ACTION OR DEFENSE

Page 391, insert in Note on Tax Claims:

Pasquantino v. United States, 544 U.S. 349 (2005), held that defendants could be prosecuted under the federal wire fraud statute for actions in the U.S. that were part of a scheme to defraud Canada and the Province of Ontario of excise duties and tax revenues applicable to the importation and sale of liquor. The Court stated: "The present prosecution is unlike these classic examples of actions traditionally barred by the revenue rule. It is not a suit that recovers a foreign tax liability, like a suit to enforce a judgment. This is a criminal prosecution brought by the United States in its sovereign capacity to punish domestic criminal conduct." Id. at 1775. "[T]his prosecution poses little risk of causing the principal evil against which the revenue rule was traditionally thought to guard: judicial evaluation of the policy-laden enactments of other sovereigns.... True, a prosecution like this one requires a court to recognize foreign law to determine whether the defendant violated U.S. law. But we may assume that by electing to bring this prosecution, the Executive has assessed this prosecution's impact on this Nation's relationship with Canada, and concluded that it poses little danger of causing international friction. We know of no common-law court that has applied the revenue rule to bar an action accompanied by such a safeguard...." Id. at 1779.

With regard to cases like Attorney General of Canada v. R.J. Reynolds Holdings, discussed in the Note, the Court stated: "We express no view on the related question whether a foreign government, based on wire or mail fraud predicate offenses, may bring a civil action under the Racketeer Influenced and Corrupt Organizations Act for a scheme to defraud it of taxes." Id. at 1771 n.1. A case that the Court had remanded for reconsideration in the light of *Pasquantino*, European Community v. RJR Nabisco, Inc., 424 F.3d 175 (2d Cir. 2005), cert. denied, ___ U.S. ___, 126 S.Ct. 1045 (2006), reaffirmed its earlier ruling that various foreign sovereigns could not recover under RICO against cigarette companies that allegedly directed and facilitated the smuggling of contraband cigarettes depriving the plaintiffs of duties and taxes not paid on the cigarettes. The Second Circuit stated: "The present civil lawsuit [unlike *Pasquantino*] is brought by foreign governments, not by the United States. Moreover, the executive branch has given us no signal that it consents to this litigation. * * * In short, the factors that led the *Pasquantino* Court to hold the revenue rule inapplicable to [wire fraud] smuggling prosecutions are missing here." Id. at 181.

SECTION 2. NOTICE AND PROOF OF FOREIGN LAW

Page 398, insert in Note 3:

In Germany, the Netherlands, and Belgium courts must apply foreign law on their own motion if the facts indicate that under the forum's choice-of-law rules foreign law controls. See Sofie Geeroms, Foreign Law In Civil Litigation 43–49, 213–216 (2004).

SECTION 3. USE OF THE FORUM'S "PROCEDURAL" RULES

A. INTRODUCTION

Page 410, insert before Note 7 and renumber Note 7 as Note 5:

Harding v. Wealands

House of Lords, 2006.
[2006] 3 W.L.R. 83.

[Mr. Harding, an Englishman, and Ms. Wealands, an Australian, formed a relationship in Australia. She came to England to live with him. Ms. Wealands returned to Australia to attend a family wedding. He later joined her for a holiday and to visit her parents. While she was driving in New South Wales (NSW) with Mr. Harding as a passenger, she lost control and the car turned over. He was badly injured and is tetraplegic. Ms. Wealands owned the vehicle and carried liability insurance issued by an Australian company. Both Mr. Harding and Ms. Wealands returned to England.

A NSW statute places limits on compensation for various damages including lost earnings and non-economic damages, and in other ways restricts recovery. Under NSW law the plaintiff would recover about 30% less than under English law. Part III of the United Kingdom Private International Law Act 1995 (main volume pages 513–14) abolishes the double actionability choice-of-law rule* for torts and creates a presumption that the law of the place of injury governs unless it is "substantially more appropriate" to apply some other law. Section 14(3)(b) states that the statute does not authorize "questions of procedure in any proceedings to be determined otherwise than in accordance with the law of the forum."

Mr. Harding sued Ms. Wealands in the High Court of Justice in London. That court ruled that English law determined the damages. The

---

* The double actionability rule, as modified in Chaplin v. Boys (main volume p. 513), state that in order for a tort to be actionable in an English court it had to be actionable under both the law of the English forum and the law of the place of the wrong. Eds.

judge gave two reasons: (1) damages were "procedural"; (2) even if damages were substantive it was "substantially more appropriate" to apply English law. The Court of Appeal allowed the appeal and applied Australian law. The three justices were agreed that it was not more appropriate to apply English law, but one justice considered the NSW statutory limits on recovery as "procedural" and therefore not applicable in England. The House of Lords, five Law Lords participating, unanimously allowed the appeal and restored the judgment of the trial court on the ground that damages were procedural.]

LORD HOFFMAN

My Lords, the issue is whether damages for personal injury caused by negligent driving in New South Wales should be calculated according to the applicable law selected in accordance with Part III of the Private International Law (Miscellaneous Provisions) Act 1995 ("Part III") or whether it is a question of procedure which falls to be determined in accordance with English law. * * *

Mr Haddon–Cave, who appeared for the claimant, said that if the House thought that the language of section 14 ["procedure"] was ambiguous or obscure, it should resolve the ambiguity by reference to a statement made in Parliament by the Lord Chancellor during the passage of the Bill. For my part, I do not think that there is any ambiguity or obscurity. Of course, taken out of context, the word "procedure" is ambiguous. In its narrow and perhaps most usual sense it means, as La Forest J expressed it in Tolofson v. Jensen [1994] 3 SCR 1022, 1072 [Supreme Court of Canada] those rules which "make the machinery of the forum court run smoothly as distinguished from those determinative of the rights of both parties." Or it can have a wider meaning which embraces what Mason CJ in Stevens v. Head (1993) 176 CLR 433, 445 [High Court of Australia] called "the traditional equation drawn between matters relating to a remedy and matters of procedure." This is the sense it which the term has always been used in English private international law. If section 14 is read in its context, against the background of the existing rules of common law and the report of the Law Commission [which preceded the enactment of the Private International Law Act], there can be no doubt that the latter meaning was intended. For my part, therefore, I see no need for Mr Haddon–Cave to resort to Hansard [report of proceedings in Parliament].

If, however, there had been any ambiguity which needed to be resolved, I am bound to say that this is as clear a case ... as anyone could hope to find. At the Report stage in the House of Lords, Lord Howie of Troon put down an amendment to add a further paragraph to what is now section 14(3), so that it would read: "[nothing in this Part] (d) authorises any court of the forum to award damages other than in accordance with the law of the forum." Lord Howie declared an interest on behalf of Cape Industries plc, which had a few years earlier been sued in Texas for asbestos-related injuries and was anxious that Part III should not import American scales of compensation into English courts. In the debate on 27 March 1995 Lord Mackay of Clashfern LC [Lord Chancellor] made what was obviously a carefully prepared statement:

> With regard to damages, issues relating to the quantum or measure of damages are at present and will continue under Part III to be governed by the law of the forum; in other words, by the law of one of the three jurisdictions in the United Kingdom. Issues of this kind are regarded as procedural and, as such, are covered by clause 14(3)(b). It follows from this that the kind of awards to which the noble Lord referred of damages made in certain states, in particular in parts of the United States, will not become a feature of our legal system by virtue of Part III. Our courts will continue to apply our own rules on quantum of damages even in the context of a tort case where the court decides that the "applicable law" should be some foreign system of law so far as concerns the merits of the claim. Some aspects of the law of damages are not regarded as procedural and, in accordance with the views of the Law Commissions in their report on the subject, Part III does not alter this. These aspects concern so-called "heads of damages"—the basic matter which is being compensated for—such as special damage relating to direct financial loss. Whether a particular legal system permits such a head of damage is not regarded as procedural but substantive and therefore not automatically subject to the law of the forum. This seems right given the intimate connection between such a concept and the particular nature of the case in issue. But again, I foresee no significant increase in awards of damages because a particular head of damage permitted by some foreign system of law would continue, so far as the quantum allocated to it in any finding is concerned, to be regulated by our own domestic law of damages. I hope the noble Lord will feel reassured.

* * * My Lords, the next question is whether the provisions of [the NSW statute that imposes limits on damages] should be characterised as relating to the actionability of the economic and non-economic damage suffered by Mr. Harding or to the remedies which the courts of New South Wales provide for such damage. On this point we could not have better authority than that of the High Court of Australia in Stevens v. Head 176 CLR 433. The majority (Brennan, Dawson, Toohey and McHugh JJ) analysed the equivalent damages-limitation provisions of the Motor Accidents Act 1988 and concluded that they were concerned with quantification rather than heads of damage. Although [the current NSW legislation] is more restrictive of the court's power to award damages than the 1988 Act, the character of the relevant provisions is in my opinion the same. * * *

[Three judges dissented in Stevens v. Head.] But there is nothing in the dissenting judgments by Mason CJ and Deane and Gaudron JJ to suggest that, if they had accepted that the court should apply the traditional distinction between actionability and remedy, including quantification of damages, they would have disagreed with the way the majority characterised the provisions of the 1988 Act. It was the traditional distinction itself which the minority rejected. Thus Mason CJ proposed that the court should adopt "a new criterion for the substance-procedure distinction which ... characterise[s] as procedural 'those rules which are directed to governing or regulating the mode or conduct of court proceedings.' All other provisions or rules are to be classified as substantive." * * *

But Mr Palmer, who appeared for the defendant [in this case] submitted that in English private international law a limit or "cap" on the damages recoverable is regarded as substantive. There is, it is true, some authority for this proposition. The 7th edition (1958) of Dicey's Conflict of Laws edited by Dr JHC Morris, contained the statement, at p 1092, "statutory provisions limiting a defendant's liability are prima facie substantive; but the true construction of the statute may negative this view." * * *

In my opinion the proposition in Dicey was too widely stated. Cope v. Doherty [(1858) 4 K & J 367, which Dicey cites] is authority for the proposition that a contractual term which limits the obligation to pay damages for a breach of contract or a tort, or a statutory provision which is deemed to operate as such a term, qualifies the substantive obligation. It is not part of the rules of the lex fori for the assessment of damages. * * *

There is accordingly in my opinion no English authority to cast any doubt upon the conclusion of the Australian High Court in Stevens v. Head that, for the purposes of the traditional distinction between substance and procedure which treats remedy as a matter of procedure, all the provisions of [the Australian legislation], including limitations on quantum, should be characterised as procedural. * * * In John Pfeiffer Pty Ltd v. Rogerson (2000) 203 CLR 503, however, the High Court reversed itself, abandoned the traditional rule (at least for torts committed in Australia) and confined the role of the leges fori of the Australian states to procedure in the narrow sense of rules "governing or regulating the mode or conduct of court proceedings." This change was said to be required by constitutional imperatives of Australian federalism. In a later decision (Regie Nationale des Usines Renault SA v. Zhang (2002) 210 CLR 491, 520, para 76) the court left open the question of whether it would apply to foreign torts. But the decision in the Pfeiffer case clearly influenced the judgments of the majority in the Court of Appeal in this case. * * *

There can however be no doubt about the general rule, stated by Lord Mackay in the House of Lords debate, that "issues relating to the quantum or measure of damages" are governed by the lex fori. And this was the rule which Parliament intended to preserve.

Even if there appeared to be more logic in the principle in Pfeiffer's case ... the question is not what the law should be but what Parliament thought it was in 1995. * * *

In my opinion, therefore, Elias J [the High Court trial judge] was right to treat the [NSW statutory] restrictions as entirely inapplicable. In the circumstances it is unnecessary to decide whether, if they had been properly characterised as substantive, it was open to the Court of Appeal to reverse his judgment that it was substantially more appropriate to apply English law. The hypothesis necessary to raise this question is in my view somewhat artificial, because most of the reasons why it may be more appropriate to apply English law are the reasons why the assessment of damages is traditionally characterised as a matter for the lex fori. I would therefore prefer not to express a view on this question. In my opinion the appeal should be allowed and the judgment of Elias J restored.

LORD ROGER OF EARLFERRY

* * * The passage which Lord Hoffmann has quoted from the Hansard report of the speech of Lord Mackay of Clashfern LC in reply to the probing amendment in the name of Lord Howie of Troon, confirms the construction which I would, in any event, have placed on the words in section 14(3)(b). But more importantly, perhaps, it shows that Parliament was assured that the provision would prevent damages being awarded by reference to the law and standards of other countries. The particular problem raised by Lord Howie related to the high level of damages in the United States which he was anxious should not be replicated here. But it would be equally unacceptable if, say, United Kingdom courts had to award damages according to a statutory scale which, while adequate in another country because of the relatively low cost of services etc. there, would be wholly inadequate in this country, having regard to the cost of the corresponding items here. As Parliament was assured by the Lord Chancellor, section 14(3)(b) guards against such eventualities. The interpretation advocated by the defendant would undermine the basis on which Parliament legislated. * * *

LORD WOOLF

* * * The limits on the amount of damages on which the defendant seeks to rely are contained in the Motor Accidents Compensation Act 1999 of New South Wales. That Act contains in Chapters 3, 4, 5 and 6 a detailed statutory procedural code containing the machinery for recovering compensation for motor accident injuries, including the way damages are to be assessed. The code is clearly one that has provisions which it would be very difficult, if not impossible, to apply in proceedings brought in this country, even though they may be capable of being applied in other parts of Australia. To have different parts of that code dealt with by different systems of law would not be an attractive result and in some cases this would produce an impractical result. (See for example section 132 which requires, in the case of a dispute over non economic loss, for the degree of impairment to be assessed by a medical assessor in New South Wales.) The greater part of the code is clearly procedural and those parts which could be

arguably regarded as substantive should be treated as being procedural as well. * * *

NOTES

1. The excerpt from the Parliamentary proceedings quoted by Lord Hoffman focuses on avoiding introducing "American scales of compensation into English Courts." Does this policy also apply to rejecting statutory limits on damages that would reduce recovery below the English standard? Lord Roger of Earlferry addresses this distinction. Does his opinion support treating the NSW limits on recovery as procedural? Does his opinion support applying English law as the substantive law that is "substantially more appropriate" in the light of England's contacts with the parties? Does the fact that Ms. Wealands carried liability insurance issued by an Australian company detract from the appropriateness of applying English law?

2. Lord Hoffman cites the opinion of the High Court of Australia in Stevens v. Head as precedent for his procedural characterization of the NSW statutory limitations on damages. Lord Hoffman notes that the High Court of Australia overruled Stevens v. Head in John Pfeiffer Pty Ltd. v. Rogerson, but he dismisses this overruling as "required by constitutional imperatives of Australian federalism." Pfeiffer states:

> Within a federal nation such as Australia, the capacity of a party to legal proceedings to choose the forum within which to bring such proceedings can be one of the advantages of the interconnected polity. However, such a facility ought not to involve the capacity of one party seriously to prejudice the legal rights of an opponent. * * *
>
> It may be reasonable to recognise the right of a litigant to choose different courts in the one nation by reason of their advantageous procedures, better facilities or greater expedition. However, it is not reasonable that such a choice, made unilaterally by the initiating party, should materially alter that party's substantive legal entitlements to the disadvantage of its opponents. If this could be done, the law would no longer provide a certain and predictable norm, neutrally applied as between the parties. Instead, it would afford a variable rule which particular parties could manipulate to their own advantage. Such a possibility would be obstructive to the integrity of a federal nation, the reasonable expectations of those living within it and the free mobility of people, goods and services within its borders upon the assumption that such movement would not give rise to a significant alteration of accrued legal rights.

203 C.L.R. 552–553.

Does this statement from *Pfeiffer* express a peculiar requirement of the Australian Constitution or does it reflect sound general choice-of-law principles?

3. United States courts have treated statutory limits on recovery as substantive. See, e.g., Marmon v. Mustang Aviation, 430 S.W.2d 182, 194 (Tex. 1968) (applying Colorado statutory limit on wrongful death recovery). Some cases have treated as substantive a court's statement of a limit on recovery. See Cunningham v. Quaker Oats Co., 107 F.R.D. 66, 73 (W.D.N.Y. 1985), which treats as substantive a statement by the Supreme Court of Canada that $100,000 should be the upper limit of non-pecuniary damages. Subsequent Canadian cases have adjusted this amount for inflation.

4. A draft regulation of the European Parliament and the Council on the Law Applicable to Non–Contractual Obligations (Rome II), Official Journal C 289E, 28/11/2006 p. 68, which seems ready for enactment in 2007, contains the following provisions:

Article 1(3):

This Regulation shall not apply to evidence and procedure, without prejudice to Articles 21 [choice of law for the formal validity of a unilateral act relating to a non-contractual obligation] and 22 [Regulation's choice-of-law provisions apply to "rules which raise presumption of law or determine the burden of proof"].

Article 15: Scope of the Law Applicable

The law applicable to non-contractual obligations under this Regulation shall govern in particular ... (c) the existence, the nature and the assessment of damage or the remedy claimed.

Do these provisions abrogate the rule that quantification of damages is procedural? The United Kingdom has agreed to be bound by Rome II.

C.   RULES OF EVIDENCE: PRIVILEGE

Page 418, insert in Note 1:

State v. Heaney, 689 N.W.2d 168 (Minn. 2004). Heaney was the driver of a vehicle that rolled over in Minnesota killing one of the passengers. Heaney was taken to a nearby hospital in Wisconsin where, against his objections, a sample of his blood was taken, which indicated intoxication. Under Wisconsin law there was no doctor-patient privilege that would prevent admission of the evidence in a criminal trial, but Minnesota law barred the evidence. At Heaney's criminal trial in Minnesota, the judge suppressed the blood-alcohol evidence. Held: reversed:

Applying the Restatement approach to this case, the state with the most significant relationship to the communication is the state where the communication occurred unless there is a prior relationship between the parties to the communication. Id. § 139 cmt. e. Here, the communication occurred in Wisconsin, the state with the most significant relationship to the communication, and there was no prior relationship between the hospital and Heaney. Furthermore, there is no strong public policy reason in Minnesota for excluding the evidence. On the contrary, the state's interest in prosecuting those who violate the state's criminal vehicular operation laws counsels admission of the evidence.

Id. at 176–77.

D.   TIME LIMITATION

Page 420, insert in Note:

Wenke v. Gehl Co., 682 N.W.2d 405 (Wis. 2004). Plaintiff was injured in Iowa while using a baler manufactured by the defendant, a Wisconsin corporation. An Iowa statute bars commencing a product liability action more than 15 years after a product "was first purchased." Plaintiff's injury occurred more than 15 years after defendant had sold the baler to an Iowa buyer. Unable to maintain the action in

Iowa, plaintiff sued in Wisconsin. The Wisconsin borrowing statute provides: "If an action is brought in this state on a foreign cause of action and the foreign period of limitation which applies has expired, no action may be maintained in this state." Held: The action is barred in Wisconsin because "the phrase 'period of limitation' ... pertains equally to foreign statutes of limitation and foreign statutes of repose." Id. at 409.

Page 426, insert in Note 2:

Nierman v. Hyatt Corp., 808 N.E.2d 290 (Mass. 2004). Plaintiff, a Massachusetts resident, made reservations through a Massachusetts travel agent for a stay a defendant's hotel in Texas. Plaintiff was injured at the hotel while climbing aboard a transport cart operated by a hotel employee. Texas has a 2–year statute of limitations for torts; Massachusetts a 3–year limitation. Plaintiff sued more than 2 years but less than 3 years after the injury. Held: applying Restatement § 142, the Texas limitation applies and the action is barred:

> We begin by noting that the more significant relationship test points clearly toward use of the Texas limitations statute. All of the events constituting the alleged negligence took place in Texas, and Texas is where the alleged injuries were suffered. Hyatt, although not a Texas corporation, operates a business there and employs Texans. The operator of the transport cart, presumably, lives in Texas. Although the Niermans are Massachusetts residents, they had traveled to Texas when the alleged accident occurred. The fact that their travel reservations were booked through Massachusetts travel agents carries no weight in our analysis, because that contact has no apparent bearing on any issue in the case, let alone the limitations issue. See Restatement (Second) of Conflict of Laws, supra at § 142 comment e (emerging trend is to bar claim if barred by "the state which, *with respect to the issue of limitations*, is the state of most significant relationship to the occurrence and to the parties stated in § 6" [emphasis supplied]).

> We next consider whether, regardless that Texas is the State with the closer connections to the issue, Massachusetts has any substantial interest that would be advanced by entertaining the Niermans' claims. We conclude that it does not. Massachusetts has a general interest in having its residents compensated for personal injuries suffered in another State. It cannot be said, however, that its interest in the timeliness of such an action is more compelling than that of Texas.

Id. at 293.

SECTION 4. REFERENCE TO THE CHOICE–OF–LAW RULES OF ANOTHER JURISDICTION

Page 449, add to the end of Note 3:

The Supreme Court focused on the physical manifestation of the wrongful conduct for purposes of applying the "foreign country" exception to the Federal Tort Claims Act. That Act exempts the government from liability for "[a]ny claim arising in a foreign country." 28 U.S.C.A. § 1350. In Sosa v. Alvarez–Machain, 542 U.S. 692 (2004) the Supreme Court confronted the scope of that exception. U.S. law enforcement came to believe that Alvarez–Machain had played a role in the torture and killing of a DEA agent in Mexico. It was arranged that Alvarez–Machain would be kidnaped in Mexico and brought to the U.S. to stand trial. He was eventually acquitted and brought a tort action against the federal government. Taking a strictly territorial view of the matter, the Court held that the "foreign country" exception applied and that he could not state a claim under the Federal Tort Claims Act. The Court rejected lower court authority that had developed the so-called "headquarters" doctrine which allowed recovery if the place of the decision that led to the tortious consequences was in the U.S.

CHAPTER 8

CHOOSING THE RULE OF DECISION

SECTION 1. THE RECEIVED SYSTEM AND TRADITION

B. EXAMPLES OF THE SYSTEM IN OPERATION

1. UNILATERAL AND MULTILATERAL APPROACHES

Page 455, insert in last paragraph of text:

People v. Laino, 87 P.3d 27 (Cal. 2004), cert. denied, 543 U.S. 886 (2004), held that for the purposes of California's "three strikes law," which provides for enhanced punishment of a convicted person who has had prior felony convictions, defendant's guilty plea in Arizona to aggravated assault against his wife counted as a prior felony conviction. Moreover, the Full Faith and Credit Clause of the U.S. Constitution did not preclude a California court from so treating the Arizona plea even though, after defendant successfully completed a domestic violence prevention program, an Arizona court entered a judgment dismissing the aggravated assault charge.

2. TRADITIONAL RULES

Page 458, insert as Note 4:

4. Rationis Enterprises Inc. of Panama v. Hyundai Mipo Dockyard Co., 426 F.3d 580 (2d Cir. 2005): Defendant shipyard modified plaintiff's ship in Korea. Because of defective welding during the modification, the ship sank on the high seas. Choice of law was governed by the factors set out in Lauritzen v. Larsen (infra Casebook p. 638). The court held that Korean law applied under which a statute of repose barred the claim. Korean law applied because the first *Lauritzen* factor is "place of the wrongful act." "[T]he place of the wrongful act is not where the vessel sinks, but where negligence occurs. The reason for this rule is not difficult to discern because it is the state where the negligence occurs that has the greatest interest in regulating the behavior of the parties." Id. at 587.

SECTION 2. ESCAPE DEVICES

A. CHARACTERIZATION

2. NATURE OF THE ACTION

Page 487, insert as Note 3:

3. There will be much less occasion to determine the extraterritorial application of a statute like those in notes 1 and 2. As part of its continuing program of "tort reform", Congress has enacted legislation nullifying any state law that imposes vicarious liability on motor vehicle rental companies. PL 109–59, 119 Stat. 1444 § 10208, amending 49 U.S.C. (August 10, 2005).

B.   RENVOI

Page 489, insert in Note 2:

The problem of what law applies to the construction of an insurance contract arises frequently with regard to underinsured motorist coverage. Courts differ as to whether the governing law is that of the state where the insured vehicle is principally garaged and where the policy was issued or is that of the state where the insured suffered injury. See, e.g. Mikelson v. United Services Auto. Assoc., 111 P.3d 601, 609 (Haw. 2005) (law of Hawaii, where insured injured, applies to permit recovery not available under law of California where policy issued—"Hawai'i has a strong interest in protecting those injured within its borders"); Champagne v. Ward, 893 So.2d 773, 789 (La. 2005) (law of Mississippi, where policy issued, applies to reduce coverage of insured injured in Louisiana—"Mississippi has a more substantial interest in the uniform application of its laws governing insurance contracts than Louisiana has in providing an insurance remedy to an out-of-state resident who was injured while transitorily within the borders of Louisiana"); Johnson v. United States Fidelity & Guaranty Co., 696 N.W.2d 431, 443 (Neb. 2005) (insured recovers under law of Nebraska where policy issued when recovery would be barred under law of Colorado where insured injured—"the application of Nebraska's laws to resolve the enforceability of contract coverage provisions between Nebraska insurers and insureds enhances the predictability of the parties' contractual rights and obligations by removing the constant variable of different states in which insureds travel").

C.   PUBLIC POLICY

Page 493, insert in Note 3:

Dowis v. Mud Slingers, Inc., 621 S.E.2d 413, 419 (Ga. 2005), expressly rejects "governmental interest" analysis, Leflar, and the Second Restatement: "The relative certainty, predictability, and ease of the application of lex loci delicti, even though sometimes leading to results which may appear harsh, are preferable to the inconsistency and capriciousness that the replacement choice-of-law approaches have wrought." Is the occasional use of "public policy," as in *Alexander*, consistent with "certainty, predictability, and ease of the application"?

SECTION 4.   THE NEW ERA

A.   ADOPTING NEW CHOICE-OF-LAW RULES

Page 511, insert in Note 3:

A draft regulation of the European Parliament and the Council on the Law Applicable to Non–Contractual Obligations (Rome II), Official Journal C 289E, 28/11/2006 p. 68, which seems ready for enactment in 2007, contains the following provision:

Article 17: Rules of Safety and Conduct

In assessing the conduct of the person claimed to be liable, account shall be taken, as a matter of fact and in so far as is appropriate, of the rules of safety and conduct which were in force at the place and time of the event giving rise to the liability.

Paragraph 30 of the recitals preceding the text of the Regulation states:

The term "rules of safety and conduct" should be interpreted as referring to all regulations having any relation to safety and conduct, including, for example, road safety rules in the case of an accident.

Is this provision broad enough to cover whether a violation of a rule of conduct is negligence per se, as in the Louisiana Conflicts Code?

Page 512, insert as Note 5:

5. Rule 8.5(b) of the Model Rules of Professional Conduct of the American Bar Association provides:

In any exercise of the disciplinary authority of this jurisdiction, the rules of professional conduct to be applied shall be as follows:

(1) for conduct in connection with a matter pending before a tribunal, the rules of the jurisdiction in which the tribunal sits, unless the rules of the tribunal provide otherwise; and

(2) for any other conduct, the rules of the jurisdiction in which the lawyer's conduct occurred, or, if the predominant effect of the conduct is in a different jurisdiction, the rules of that jurisdiction shall be applied to the conduct. A lawyer shall not be subject to discipline if the lawyer's conduct conforms to the rules of a jurisdiction in which the lawyer reasonably believes the predominant effect of the lawyer's conduct will occur.

CHANGES IN THE CONFLICTS RULES OF OTHER COUNTRIES
Page 516, insert after Hungary:

Quebec

Civil Code of Quebec, Book 10, Title 2, Ch. III, Sect. II, § 10 s.3126:

The obligation to make reparation for injury caused to another is governed by the law of the country where the injurious act occurred. However, if the injury appeared in another country, the law of the latter country is applicable if the person who committed the injurious act should have foreseen that the damage would occur.

In any case where the person who committed the injurious act and the victim have their domiciles or residences in the same country, the law of that country applies.

Page 516, insert in text:

A draft regulation of the European Parliament and the Council on the Law Applicable to Non–Contractual Obligations (Rome II), Official Journal C 289E, 28/11/2006 p. 68, which seems ready for enactment in 2007, contains the following provision:

Article 4: General Rule

1. Unless otherwise provided for in this Regulation, the law applicable to a non-contractual obligation arising out of a tort/delict shall be the law of the country in which the damage occurs irrespective of the country in which the event giving rise to the damage occurred and irrespective of the country or countries in which the indirect consequences of that event occur.

2. However, where the person claimed to be liable and the person sustaining damage both have their habitual residence in the same country at the time when the damage occurs, the law of that country shall apply.

3. Where it is clear from all the circumstances of the case that the tort/delict is manifestly more closely connected with a country other than that indicated in paragraphs 1 or 2, the law of that other country shall apply. A manifestly closer connection with another country might be based in particular on a pre-existing relationship between the parties, such as a contract, that is closely connected the tort/delict in question.

What is the meaning of "manifestly more closely connected" in 4(3)? Would it prevent 4(2) from producing the result in Haynie v. Hanson, discussed in Note 1 Casebook p. 484?

The current draft regulation (see also change to Casebook p. 1072, infra this Supplement) like previous drafts and unlike § 145 of the Restatement (Second), does not provide or envision dépeçage. It calls for the application of a single law. See also infra Casebook p. 1097, comment (d). See also, infra this Supplement to Casebook p. 1086. Query whether resort (deference) to a single (!) more closely connected other law is enough to accommodate competing social ("governmental") interests?

Pages 518–519, replace material on Japan with:

Traditional Japanese conflicts law (the *Horei* on the Application of Laws (1998)) closely followed its German model. Contrary to the latter, however, it contained a provision dealing with non-contractual obligations, i.e. treating together (Art. 11) obligations arising from tort, unjust enrichment, and acting on behalf of another. (For the last of these, see infra this Supplement, Note 6a to Casebook p. 1100): the applicable law was the law of the place "where the facts giving rise to the claim occurred." Art. 11(1). Some decisions, like their American counterparts, disapproved of the mechanical application of the application of the law fortuitous place of where the accident occurred and looked to other, more relevant connecting factors, such as the place of conduct, the parties' common nationality or domicile, places of business, and the like. See Masanobu Ito v. Thai Airways International Public Co. Ltd., [2001] H.J. (1745) 102 (Tokyo Dist. Ct. 2000), transl. in 45 Japanese Ann. Int'l L. 164 (2002).

After years of study and debate, Japan adopted a new "Act on the General Rules of Application of Laws" [*Ho no Tekiyo ni Kansuru Tsusoku-ho*] in June 2006, effective Jan. 1, 2007. For translations, see 8 Yb. Private Int'l L. ____ (expected June 2007) and Anderson & Okuda, [2006] Asian–Pacific L. & Pol. J. 138 (2006). For a German translation, see [2006] Zeitschrift für Rechtsvergleichung 227 (Austria, 2006).The new statute is now closer to current European law, for instance, by having special rules for consumer and employment contracts (for Europe, see infra Casebook pp. 1083–1085).

The new statute, like the proposed European Community Rome–II Regulation (see additions to Casebook p. 1086 et seq., infra this Supplement p. 55 et seq.), now differentiates among the different kinds of non-contractual obligations: For claims arising from acting on behalf of another (see above) and unjust enrichment, the statute directs application of the law of the state where the facts giving rise to the claim took place (Art. 14); for tort (and contrary to proposals calling for application of the law of the place of conduct), Art. 17, like the proposed European law (above), focuses on the law of the place of injury. In both cases, the court may apply a more closely connected law (for instance, because of a preexisting relationship between the parties or, in tort, because of their common domicile; see Arts. 15 and 20, respectively).

Page 519, Insert as a new first paragraph in the Note:

For discussion of the draft project, see also Zvekov, "The New Civil Code of the Russian Federation and Private International Law," 44 McGill L.J. 525 (1999). The new Russian conflicts law entered into force on March 1, 2002, as chapter VI of Part Three of the Civil Code: Part Three and an introductory law of Nov. 26, 2001, Nos. 146–FZ and 147–FZ, SZRF 2001, No. 48, positions 4552 and 4553, respectively, as cited by A. Mayer and B. Breig, Das internationale Privatrecht im Zivilgesetzbuch der Russischen Föderation, 14 Zeitschrift für Europäisches Privatrecht 829 n. 2 (2006). The torts provision, quoted above in draft, has remained unchanged, but has become Art. 1219. Id. at 848. Special provisions address products liability (Art. 1221), unfair competition (Art. 1222), and unjust enrichment (1223). Id. at 849–50.

Page 529, insert as new paragraph at the end of Note 1:

Subsection (d) limits the parties' freedom of choice in the context of consumer contracts. Compare this provision with the similar consumer-protective rule in Art. 5 of the Rome Convention, applicable among European Union countries: infra p. 1083. An exception in favor of consumers is not yet part of all modern movements codifying choice-of-law rules in contract. See, e.g., Art. 47 of the Model Law on Private International Law of the People's Republic of China (6th draft, 2000), which only requires a factual connection to the chosen court and excludes cases for which the Model Law specifies that particular courts have exclusive jurisdiction. Among the latter, interestingly, are disputes arising from joint Chinese-foreign ventures. Art. 31 confers jurisdiction on PRC courts for actions brought by consumers domiciled or habitually resident in the PRC, but does not address the issue raised here with respect to choice-of-law clauses.

Page 533, insert in text before Note 1:

The Contract Law of the Peoples' Republic of China provides:

> The parties to a contract involving foreign interests may choose the law applicable to the settlement of their contract disputes, except as otherwise stipulated by law. If the parties to a contract involving foreign interests have not made a choice, the law of the country to which the contract is most closely connected shall be applied.
>
> The contracts for Chinese-foreign equity joint ventures, for Chinese-foreign contractual joint ventures and for Chinese-foreign cooperative exploration and development of natural resources to be performed within the territory of the People's Republic of China shall apply the laws of the People's Republic of China.
>
> Contract Law art. 126 (adopted at the Second Session of the Ninth People's Congress, March 15, 1999).

See similarly, Arts. 100–101 of the Model Law of Private International Law of the People's Republic of China (Chinese Society of Private International Law of the People's Republic of China, Beijing: The Law Press, 6th draft, 2000): the provisions (with emphasis on the "closest connection") very much resemble (draw upon) the Rome Convention model.

The new Japanese conflicts statute (supra this Supplement pp. 31–32, changes to Casebook pp. 518–519), provides, with great generality, that formation and validity of the parties' choice of law are governed by the chosen law: Art. 7 (see similarly Art. 3(4) of the Rome Convention in the European Community, infra p. 1074). Obviously, the freedom of choice is not unfettered. As in European law, there are restrictions to protect consumers (Art. 11), employees (Art. 12), and in favor of local public policy (Arts. 22, 42).

Page 533, insert in Note 1:

A draft regulation of the European Parliament and the Council on the Law Applicable to Non–Contractual Obligations (Rome II), Official Journal C 289E, 28/11/2006 supra Casebook p. 68 (see also infra Supplement p. 59), which seems ready for enactment in 2007, contains the following provision:

> Article 14 Freedom of choice
>
> 1. The parties may agree to submit non-contractual obligations to the law of their choice:
>
> (a) by an agreement entered into after the event giving rise to the damage occurred; or
>
> (b) where all the parties are pursuing a commercial activity, also by an agreement freely negotiated before the event giving rise to the damage occurred.
>
> The choice shall be expressed or demonstrated with reasonable certainty by the circumstances of the case and shall not prejudice the rights of third parties.
>
> 2. Where all the elements relevant to the situation at the time when the event giving rise to the damage occurs, are located in a country

other than the country whose law has been chosen, the choice of the parties shall not prejudice the application of provisions of the law of that country which cannot be derogated from by agreement.

3. Where all the elements relevant to the situation at the time when the event giving rise to the damage occurs, are located in one or more of the Member States, the parties' choice of the law applicable other than that of a Member State shall not prejudice the application of provisions of Community law, where appropriate as implemented in the Member State of the forum, which cannot be derogated from by agreement.

Page 533, Note 1, insert in Note 1, after sentence ending in 5th line:

Accord: Olinick v. BMG Entertainment, 42 Cal.Rptr.3d 268 (Cal.App. 2 Dist. 2006), rev. denied (Aug. 16, 2006). Additional cases reaching this result are collected in S. Symeonides, Choice of Law in American Courts in 2006: 20th Annual Survey, ___ Am.J. Comp.L. ___, ___ n. 347 (2006). For decisions reaching a contrary result (main text), see id., 2nd para.

Page 534, insert at the end of Note 1:

In most cases, in contrast to *Hoes* (supra note 1), courts have held that contractual choice-of-law clauses do not cover torts arising from the parties' contractual relationship. See, in particular, Williams v. Deutsche Bank Securities, Inc., 2005 WL 1414435 (S.D.N.Y. 2005). For further references, see Symeonides, Choice of Law in American Courts in 2005: Nineteenth Annual Survey, 54 Am. J.Comp.L. ___, n. 452 et seq. (2006). Accord: Or. Rev. Stat. § 81.120. As these decisions emphasize, the point is not that these clauses cannot extend beyond contract and encompass tort, but rather to determine the parties' intent. See Symeonides, supra, nn. 454–58.

Page 538, insert in Note 2:

French v. Liebmann, 440 F.3d 145 (4th Cir. 2006), cert. denied, ___ U.S. ___, 127 S.Ct. 72 (2006). Mrs. French's creditors filed an involuntary bankruptcy petition against her. Within six months of this filing, Mrs. French had transferred Bahamian real property to her children as a gift. Under U.S. bankruptcy law the trustee in bankruptcy could recover the real estate as property of the bankrupt's estate that was subject to the claims of creditors. Under Bahamian law he could not. Held: U.S. law applies.

> [T]he United States has a stronger interest than the Bahamas in regulating this transaction. The purpose of the United States Bankruptcy Code is to protect the rights of both debtors and creditors during insolvency. The Code protects debtors by providing them a fresh start. In exchange, the Code's avoidance provisions protect creditors by preserving the bankruptcy estate against illegitimate depletions. The United States has a strong interest in extending these personal protections to its residents-including the vast majority of the interested parties here. The Bahamas, by contrast, has comparatively little interest in protecting nonresidents. Thus, applying Bahamian law here would undercut the purpose of the United States Bankruptcy Code by withdrawing its protections from those it is intended to cover, while simultaneously failing to protect any Bahamian residents.

Id. at 154.

Page 539, insert in Note 3:

J. Carruthers, The Transfer of Property in the Conflict of Laws 282 (2005), suggests the following rule to govern issues arising from the transfer of realty:

> The general rule [choosing the law of the situs] shall not apply where it appears from the circumstances as a whole that the transfer or issue is more closely connected with another country ("the non-situs country"), and in such cases the applicable law for determining the issue or issues arising (as the case may be) shall be the law of that non-situs country.

Page 547, insert in Note 9:

General Motors Corp. v. Eighth Judicial District Court, 134 P.3d 111 (Nev. 2006), overrules *Motenko* and adopts the Restatement (Second) "most significant relationship test." The court rejected the *Motenko* approach because it "reduces the conflict-of-laws analysis in tort actions to a quantitative comparison of contacts, without any regard to a qualitative comparison of true conflicts-of-law between states.... The stated purpose of the *Motenko* test was to meet 'the goal of a higher degree of certainty, predictability and uniformity of result.' However, as this court's decision in Northwest Pipe Co. v. District Court demonstrates, the application of the *Motenko* test to multiparty tort actions hinders, rather than promotes, these goals." Id. at 115–116.

B.   THE COURTS AT WORK

Page 554, insert in Note:

NOTE

Jaffe v. Pallotta TeamsWorks, 374 F.3d 1223 (D.C. Cir. 2004). A D.C. resident, while on a bicycle ride in Virginia to raise funds for charity, died after receiving treatment from the University of Maryland Medical System Corporation (UMMS), which provided medical services for the ride. The decedent had signed a release that exempted UMMS from liability for negligence. Under Virginia law the release was void but its status under D.C. law was unclear. Held: Virginia law applies and the release is void. "Virginia obviously has an interest in preventing non-residents from being negligently injured or killed within its borders." Id. at 1228.

Page 560, insert at the end of Note 1:

See also Mihalic v. K–Mart of Amsterdam, N.Y., 363 F.Supp.2d 394 (N.D.N.Y. 2005): conflicting rules on contribution characterized as loss-allocating—see *Schultz*—and to be decided under the *Neumeier* rules. New York law applied as the law of the place of injury. *Neumeier* rule 3 applied as to non-New York subcontractors and Pennsylvania employers: again, state-of-injury (New York) law applied, the escape clause of rule 3 being inapplicable for lack of a predominant Pennsylvania interest.

C.   PROBLEMS EMERGED AND EMERGING

1.   PREDICTABILITY

Page 581, insert in Note 1:

Beilfuss v. Huffy Corp., 685 N.W.2d 373 (Wis. App. 2004). A former employee, residing in Wisconsin, sued his former employer, an Ohio corporation, in a Wisconsin state court seeking a declaration that provisions in the employment contract were unenforceable. The provisions limited the employee's ability to work for a competitor of the employer. The employer moved to dismiss based on provisions in the contract limiting litigation of disputes concerning the employment contract to Ohio courts and selecting Ohio law as governing the contract. The trial judge granted the motion to dismiss. Held: reversed. "[T]he choice of law provision is unenforceable because it violates Wisconsin's long-standing public policy controlling covenants not to compete, in that [the noncompetition agreements are invalid under Wisconsin and valid under Ohio law]. Moreover, we hold that because important public policy considerations are involved, it is unreasonable to enforce the forum selection provision." Id. at 379.

6. COMPLEX LITIGATION

Page 621, insert in text:

On February 18, 2005, President Bush signed into law the Class Action Fairness Act of 2005. Pub. L. No. 109–002, 119 Stat.4 (2005). The Act applies to "any civil action commenced on or after the date of enactment." § 9. It permits removal from state court and gives federal district courts original jurisdiction on the basis of minimal diversity (§ 6: "any member of a class of plaintiffs is a citizen of a State different from any defendant") of any class action in which the amount in controversy exceeds $5,000,000. Thus the plaintiffs' attorney can no longer prevent removal from state to federal court by joining a defendant of the same citizenship as any plaintiff (Strawbridge v. Curtiss, 7 U.S. (3 Cranch) 267, 2 L.Ed. 435 (1806), overruled on other grounds, Louisville R.R. v. Letson, 43 U.S. 497, 11 L.Ed. 353 (1844) (holding that for federal diversity jurisdiction to attach, complete diversity is required, each defendant being of diverse citizenship from each plaintiff)) or by suing in a state court in a state where any defendant is a citizen. (28 U.S.C. § 1441(b) provides that a case cannot be removed from state court under federal diversity jurisdiction if any defendant is a citizen of the state in which suit is brought.) The only exception to federal jurisdiction is if "greater than two-thirds of the members of all proposed plaintiff classes in the aggregate are citizens of the State in which the action was originally filed." § 4.

Although state courts will no longer be viable forums for multi-state or national class actions, the Act does not contain a choice-of-law provision. Will a federal district court have to apply the choice-of-law rules of the state in which the court is sitting or will the court be free to adopt a federal rule? See Klaxon Co. v. Stentor Elec. Mfg. Co., p. 680; Woolley, *Erie* and Choice of Law after the Class Action Fairness Act, 80 Tul. L. Rev. 1723 (2006) (*Klaxon* applies and a federal court must apply the choice-of-law rule of the forum state); Issacharoff, Settled Expectations in a World of Unsettled Law: Choice of Law after the Class Action Fairness Act, 106 Colum. L. Rev. 1839 (2006) (urging federal courts to adopt a rule applying the law of the state that was the center of defendant's wrongful acts). If a federal court must apply the conflicts rules of the forum state, where the action is filed will matter and may be the difference between certification and dismissal. See Ysbrand v. DaimlerChrysler Corp., Casebook p. 626, applying Michigan law to the warranty claims of all national class members.

Under the Class Action Fairness Act, will an attorney representing a national class improve the chances of certification by suing in a state like California (see Washington Mutual Bank v. Superior Court, Casebook p. 620) that in such actions presumes that the law of other states is the same as that of California unless the defendant shows otherwise? After removal to federal court under the Act, the federal judge will have to resolve the problem of whether on this issue the judge must follow California law or is free to apply federal procedural law, which places on the plaintiff the burden of demonstrating that in the light of variations in state law and choice-of-law analysis, "any problems with predominance or superiority can be overcome." Castano v. American Tobacco Co., 84 F.3d 734, 741 (5th Cir. 1996).

The answer is likely to be in favor of following the federal placement of burden on the plaintiff to explore variations in state laws. There is a somewhat analogous problem under Federal Rule of Civil Procedure 44.1 (p. 403), which states that when determining the law of a foreign country, the court "may consider any relevant material or source ... whether or not submitted by a party...." The Advisory Committee Notes on 44.1 state: "There is no requirement that the court give formal notice of its intention to engage in its own research on an issue of foreign law which has been raised by them, or of its intention to raise and determine independently an issue not raised by them."

Moreover, under Federal Rule of Civil Procedure 23, which requires that a class action be "efficient," that common questions of law or fact predominate, and that the class action will present no great difficulties of management, there are, pursuant to Byrd v. Blue Ridge Rural Electric Cooperative, Inc. (Casebook p. 654), "affirmative countervailing considerations" militating against the use of state presumptions. Concerns with the quality of justice administered in a federal court may justify putting the burden on the plaintiff to deal with choice of law before certification. Further, under Hanna v. Plumer (Casebook p. 659), Congress in enacting FRCP 23 and federal courts in interpreting the rule have the "power to regulate matters which, though falling within the uncertain area between substance and procedure, are rationally capable of classification as either."

In rebuttal it might be argued that the state-law presumption that other laws are the same as the forum's eliminates choice-of-law problems and assures that the requirements of Rule 23 are met insofar as they are affected by variations in state law. Nevertheless, a federal court might wish to preclude such problems from arising when addressed by the defendant and to accomplish this by placing the burden on the plaintiff at the outset. See Woolley, *Erie* and Choice of Law after the Class Action Fairness Act, 80 Tul. L. Rev. 1723, 1724 (2006): "But the claim that Rule 23 permits federal courts to ignore state law presumptions in favor of forum law is paper-thin and may not survive review by the United States Supreme Court.''

Page 627, add at the end of the top paragraph:

Similarly, an Illinois appellate court held that California law should apply (as the defendant's principal place of business and the place of the alleged tortious conduct) if a national class action were to be certified in Illinois, also rejecting defendants' constitutional objection. Barbara's Sales, Inc., et al. v. Intel Corp. et al., 857 N.E.2d 717, 723 (Ill.App. 5 Dist. 2006), appeal allowed, 861 N.E.2d 653 (Ill. 2006). For choice of law in national class actions, see also R. Weintraub, Commentary on the Conflict of Laws § 6.33, particularly at pp. 465–66 (5th ed. 2006).

In a non-class action products liability case, the Illinois appellate court applied the lex fori to the claim of a Michigan plaintiff against an Illinois defendant because "Illinois has a strong interest in applying its product liability law to regulate culpable conduct occurring within its borders, induce the design of safer products, and deter future misconduct. . . . [Illinois was the defendant's] principal place of business, the place where the [design decision and the decision] to place the product into the stream of commerce [were made]." Townsend v. Sears, Roebuck and Co., 858 N.E.2d 552, 559–60 (Ill.App. 2006). While Michigan, unlike Illinois, would not allow punitive damages, "where the purpose of disallowing punitive damages is not related to redressing the plaintiffs' injury, once the plaintiffs are made whole by recovery of . . . compensatory damages . . ., the interests of Michigan law are satisfied." Id. at 561.

7. DEPEÇAGE

Page 627, insert in text:

It is easiest to justify a result like that in *Ysbrand* when the law of the state where defendant's conduct is centered is so favorable to plaintiffs that no member of the class would recover more under the law of the member's home state. See, e.g., International Union of Operating Engineers Local #68 Welfare Fund v. Merck & Co., 2005 WL 2205341 (N.J. Super. 2005).

Reasonable persons might differ as to whether it is desirable to facilitate certification of a multi-state class action by applying to all claims the law of a single state where defendant's acts originated. Defendants often contend that it is not only unwise to do so but also unconstitutional, citing Phillips Petroleum Co. v. Shutts (Casebook p. 360). Does *Shutts* support such a claim? Phillips produced natural gas from land in eleven states. The royalty recipients brought a class action against Phillips in a Kansas state court for interest on royalty payments that Phillips had withheld pending Federal Power Commission approval of new rates. The Kansas courts held that Kansas law determined the amount of interest payable on proceeds from wells in all eleven states to recipients in fifty states, the District of Columbia, and several foreign countries. Phillips contested this ruling on due process and full faith and credit grounds. The court reversed holding that it was a violation of due process to apply Kansas law if Kansas law was more favorable to the class members than the laws of the states where the wells were located.

In *Shutts* fewer than 1,000 of the over 28,000 class members resided in Kansas and only one quarter of one per cent of the gas leases were on Kansas land. Under *Shutts* it is unconstitutional to select the law of a state where some class members live and apply that law to a national class action when that law is more favorable to class members than the laws of other states having more significant relationships with the other class members and with the defendant. Is it unconstitutional in a national class action to apply the law of a single state if that is the state where the defendant's wrongful acts were centered? Whose constitutional rights are violated? Does the state where the defendant misbehaved have an interest in punishing and deterring such conduct and is it unfair to the defendant to apply the law of that state even in favor of nonresident plaintiffs? How about those members of the class that would recover more under the law of their home state? Is unfairness to those class members eliminated if they can opt out of the action? Suppose, as is often so, that the claims of any individual class member or even of a state-wide class are so small as to make a national class action the only feasible route to recovery.

In Ysbrand v. DaimlerChrysler Corp., (Casebook p. 626) the Supreme Court of Oklahoma rejected the constitutional *Shutts* argument. In re St. Jude Medical, Inc., 425 F.3d 1116, 1120 (8th Cir. 2005), however, gave *Shutts* as the reason why it would be unconstitutional to apply the law of Minnesota, where defendant was headquartered, to the claims of class members whose home state laws differed from those of Minnesota. *See also* State Farm Mutual Auto. Ins. Co. v. Campbell, 538 U.S. 408, 421–22 (2003):

> Nor, as a general rule, does a State have a legitimate concern in imposing punitive damages to punish a defendant for unlawful acts committed outside of the State's jurisdiction. Any proper adjudication of conduct that occurred outside Utah to other persons would require their inclusion, and, to those parties, the Utah courts, in the usual case, would need to apply the laws of their relevant jurisdiction. [citing *Shutts*].

Page 632, insert in Note 6:

Kearney v. Salomon Smith Barney, Inc., 137 P.3d 914 (Cal. 2006). Plaintiffs brought a class action on behalf of California clients of the defendant, a financial institution that had its principal place of business in Georgia. Without the clients' knowledge, the defendant recorded telephone calls between the defendant's Georgia office and California clients. This was permitted under Georgia law but not under California law. The court held that California law applied. The recording of the calls without the clients' knowledge or consent constituted an unlawful invasion of privacy. The plaintiffs were entitled to injunctive relief barring defendant from such conduct in the future, but were not entitled to monetary damages or restitution for past conduct:

> Although we conclude that the comparative impairment analysis* supports the application of California law in this context, we further conclude that because one of the goals of that analysis is the "maximum attainment of underlying purpose by *all* governmental entities" (Offshore Rental [Co. v. Continental Oil Co.] 22 Cal.3d 157, 166, 148 Cal.Rptr. 867, 872, 583 P.2d 721, 726 [(1978)], italics added), it is appropriate in this instance to apply California law in a restrained manner that accommodates Georgia's reasonable interest in protecting persons who in the past might have undertaken actions in Georgia in reasonable reliance on Georgia law from being subjected to monetary liability for such actions. Prior to our resolution of this case it would have been reasonable for a business entity such as SSB to be uncertain as to which state's law-Georgia's or California's-would be applicable in this context, and the denial of monetary recovery for past conduct that might have been undertaken in reliance upon another state's law is unlikely to undermine significantly the California interest embodied in the applicable invasion-of-privacy statutes. We therefore conclude that it is Georgia's, rather than California's, interest that would be more severely impaired were monetary liability to be imposed on SSB for such past conduct. Under these circumstances, we conclude it is appropriate to decline to impose damages upon SSB (or to require it to provide restitution) on the basis of such past conduct.

Id. at 918.

* See Bernhard v. Harrah's Club, Casebook p. 589. Eds.

CHAPTER 9

CONFLICTS PROBLEMS IN FEDERAL AND INTERNATIONAL SETTINGS

SECTION 1. SPECIAL PROBLEMS IN FEDERAL COURTS

A. THE CONSTRAINTS AND TOLERANCES OF THE *ERIE* PRINCIPLE

Page 653, insert in Note 4:

But cf. S.J. v. Issaquah School Dist. No. 411, 470 F.3d 1288 (9th Cir. 2006) (in an action under federal law when there is no federal statute of limitations and a federal court borrows the state's statute of limitations, the federal rule applies, which, unlike the state rule, tolls the statute when suit is filed rather than when process is served).

Page 666, add to Note 4 at end of first paragraph (p. 666, line 3):

In Reiser v. Residential Funding Corp., 380 F.3d 1027 (7th Cir. 2004), cert. denied, 543 U.S. 1147 (2005), the court adhered to its own 16–year–old *Erie*-prediction as to how the state supreme court would answer a question of state law, despite intervening state appellate court opinions expressly rejecting that prediction, and reversed the district court which had followed the state appellate courts' view.

Page 666, add as Note 6:

6. A related problem is what some commentators refer to as the "reverse-*Erie*" problem, which is the extent to which federal procedural and quasi-procedural rules apply in the place of state rules when a state court adjudicates a federal claim. See Kevin M. Clermont, Reverse–*Erie*, 82 Notre Dame L. Rev. 1 (2006). The leading illustration of this problem is probably the Supreme Court's decision in Felder v. Casey, 487 U.S. 131 (1988). In that case, a Wisconsin state court applied a state "notice of claim" statute to a claim against police officers under 28 U.S.C. § 1983. Analogizing to the *Erie* "outcome" test that was refined in Hanna, the Court refused to allow Wisconsin state courts to apply their state statute: "Because the notice-of-claim statute at issue here conflicts in both its purpose and effects with the remedial objectives of § 1983, and because its enforcement in such actions will frequently and predictably produce different outcomes in § 1983 litigation based solely on whether the claim is asserted in state or federal court, we conclude that the state law is pre-empted when the § 1983 action is brought in a state court." *Felder*, 487 U.S. at 138.

Is the "outcome" or "twin aims" test an appropriate guide in reverse-*Erie* cases? Consider this question again as you read the material on federal questions in relation to state law, infra Casebook p. 691.

SECTION 2. CONFLICTS PROBLEMS IN INTERNATIONAL SETTINGS

A. INTERNATIONAL CONFLICTS CASES AND THE FEDERAL CONTROL OF FOREIGN AFFAIRS

Page 722, add as Note 5:

5. In Sosa v. Alvarez–Machain, 542 U.S. 692 (2004) the Supreme Court confronted another aspect of the potential applicability of the *Erie* doctrine to theories founded on international law. U.S. law enforcement came to believe that Alvarez–Machain had played a role in the torture and killing of a DEA agent in Mexico. It was arranged that Alvarez–Machain would be kidnapped in Mexico and brought to the U.S. to stand trial. He was eventually acquitted and brought a tort action against the federal government under the Federal Tort Claims Act [see insert p. 449] and against the persons responsible for his kidnapping under the Alien Tort Statute, 28 U.S.C.A. § 1350. That statute, whose origins date back to the Judiciary Act of 1789, provides: "The district courts shall have original jurisdiction of any civil action by an alien for a tort only, committed in violation of the law of nations or a treaty of the United States." The Court concluded that the statute was not only jurisdictional but also provided "a cause of action for the modest number of international law violations with a potential for personal liability at the time." Id. at 724. These violations in 1789 were "offenses against ambassadors, violations of safe conduct . . . and individual actions arising out of prize captures and piracy." Id. at 720. Nor did *Erie* prevent federal courts from allowing recovery under the statute for violations of international law that were not recognized when Congress first enacted the statute:

> *Erie* did not in terms bar any judicial recognition of new substantive rules, no matter what the circumstances, and post-*Erie* understanding has identified limited enclaves in which federal courts may derive some substantive law in a common law way. For two centuries we have affirmed that the domestic law of the United States recognizes the law of nations.

Id. at 729.

> Federal courts must, however, exercise caution in recognizing new violations of international law:

> Whatever the ultimate criteria for accepting a cause of action subject to jurisdiction under § 1350, we are persuaded that federal courts should not recognize private claims under federal common law for violations of any international law norm with less definite content and acceptance among civilized nations than the historical paradigms familiar when § 1350 was enacted.

Id. at 732.

The Court concluded that Alvarez–Machain's claim did not fall within the parameters of the statute as the wrong he asserts against his kidnappers—"a single illegal detention of less than a day"—did not qualify as a violation of international law under the Court's standard.

C. INTERNATIONAL CONFLICTS CASES IN THE ABSENCE OF FEDERAL LIMITATIONS OR PREEMPTION

Page 735, Note 5, replace paragraph beginning with 4th line on p. 735 and continuing to p. 736 with the following:

Federal Circuits differed as to whether § 6a(2)'s requirement that there be "a" Sherman Act Claim can be met by showing that a party other than the plaintiff has such a claim. Compare, e.g., Den Norske Stats Oljeselskap v. HeereMac Vof, 241 F.3d 420 (5th Cir. 2001), cert. denied, 534 U.S. 1127 (2002) (Norwegian plaintiff must assert own claim; not sufficient to show U.S. companies have claim), with Kruman v. Christie's Int'l PLC, 284 F.3d 384 (2d Cir. 2002), cert. dismissed, 539 U.S. 978, 124 S.Ct. 27 (2003) (injured third parties have standing). In F. Hoffmann–La Roche Ltd. et al. v. Empagran S.A. et al., 542 U.S. 155, 124 S.Ct. 2359 (2004), the United States Supreme Court emphasized that the Act excludes foreign anti-competitive conduct and its foreign effects: when "the adverse foreign effect is independent of any domestic effect." 124 S.Ct. at 2366. "We conclude that the exception does not apply where the plaintiff's claim rests solely on the independent foreign harm." Id. at 2363. Why not? In *Hartford,* supra at p. 733, Justice Scalia employed a comity-based choice-of-law analysis on that issue in his dissent. The *Empagran* majority picks up Justice Scalia's notions of "prescriptive comity" and concludes on the policy note that, "if America's antitrust policies could not win their own way in the international market place for such ideas, Congress, we must assume, would not have tried to impose them, in an act of legal imperialism, through legislative fiat." Id. at 2369. For comment, see Hay and Krätzschmar, in: 50 Recht der Internationalen Wirtschaft 667 (2004, in German). When is the foreign effect independent of any domestic effect or, put differently, when are they sufficiently related so that American antitrust law applies? On remand in *Empagran,* the D.C. Circuit affirmed the District Court's dismissal: there must be "a direct causal relationship" between the domestic effects and the foreign conduct. Empagran S.A. v. F. Hoffmann–LaRoche, Ltd., 417 F.3d 1267, 1271 (D.C.Cir. 2005), pet. cert. denied, ___ U.S. ___, 126 S.Ct. 1043 (2006).

Another issue of the applicability of U.S. law arose in Spector v. Norwegian Cruise Line Ltd., 545 U.S. 119, 125 S.Ct. 2169 (2005). In that case, disabled American travelers sued contending that the defendant's cruise ships did not meet the standards of the Americans with Disabilities Act ("ADA"). The defendant was a Bermuda corporation with its principal place of business in Florida. Although the cruise ships depart from and return to U.S. ports, they fly the Bahamian flag. The Court concluded that the ADA's provisions covering "public accommodations" and "specified public transportation services" were broad enough to encompass cruise ships. The Court concluded that general statutory language, such as that in the ADA, was "presumed to apply to conduct that takes place aboard a foreign-flag vessel in United States territory if the interests of the United States or its citizens, rather than interests internal to the ship, are at stake." Id. at 2177. In order for Congress to regulate the "internal order and discipline" of the ship, Congress would have to make a "clear statement" to that effect, which a majority of the Court concluded was lacking in the ADA. Id. at 2178. Thus, the Court concluded that the cruise lines would be required to make modifications in some of the procedures and policies to accommodate the disabled travelers, but would not be required to make "a permanent and significant alteration of a physical feature of the ship," id. at

2180, as mandating such alterations would in effect regulate the internal affairs of the ship.

Is *Spector* consistent with *Empagran*?

For discussion of the reach of American law in another context, see Note, Does the National Labor Relations Act Extend to Americans Who Are Temporarily Abroad?, 105 Colum. L. Rev. 2135 (2005).

CHAPTER 11

FAMILY LAW

SECTION 1. MARRIAGE

Page 811, Note 7, add at the end and insert the following new material:

See also infra Note 8, first paragraph (infra this Supplement).

In Goodridge et al. v. Department of Public Health, 440 Mass. 309, 798 N.E.2d 941 (2003), the Massachusetts Supreme Judicial Court held that the state's restriction of marriage to heterosexual couples violated the state constitution and declared general marriage law applicable to same-sex couples. Lower courts in Washington and Maryland also have held their states' versions of DOMA to violate state constitutional law. See Castle v. State, 2004 WL 1985215 (Super. Ct. Wash. 2004); Deane et al. v. Conaway et al., 2006 WL 148145 (Cir. Ct. Md. 2006). All decisions have been suspended to allow for appeal. Other courts, in contrast, have dismissed challenges on state and federal constitutional grounds to the state's DOMA. See, e.g., Wilson v. Ake, 354 F.Supp.2d 1298, 1305 (M.D.Fla. 2005) (same-sex couple, validly married in Massachusetts, sought declaratory relief to establish the validity of the marriage in Florida; petition denied).

On May 17, 2004, same-sex couples began marrying in Massachusetts. Same-sex couples residing in a state that does not permit them to marry cannot validly marry in Massachusetts. Mass. G.L. Ann. pt. II, tit. III, ch. 207 § 11. This provision, which has its counterpart in older European conflicts law that determined capacity to marry by reference to the home law (law of nationality) of the parties, is part of Massachusetts' version of the Uniform Marriage Evasion Act (supra p. 808, note 4). The Massachusetts Supreme Judicial Court upheld the application of the provision to same-sex marriages in Cote–Whitacre et al. v. Department of Pub. Health et al., 446 Mass. 350, 844 N.E.2d 623 (2006): as to plaintiffs resident in Connecticut, Maine, New Hampshire and Vermont the Court upheld the trial court's denial of injunctions to compel issuance of marriage licenses, because those states do not permit same-sex marriages. As to plaintiffs residing in New York and Rhode Island, the Court remanded for a determination of those states' law as permitting or prohibiting same-sex marriages. A curious case involved a Connecticut same-sex couple that had entered into a marriage in Massachusetts in contravention to the Massachusetts limitation. The marriage was therefore subject to annulment in Massachusetts. However, a Connecticut court held, for reasons announced in *Rosengarten*, that it lacked subject matter jurisdiction to decree an annulment. Also, the court asked, why seek an annulment when, because of Connecticut's policy at the time, the Massachusetts marriage does not exist? Lane v. Albanese, 39 Conn. L. Rptr. 3 (2005). Is restricting same-sex marriage to local residents constitutional?

Alaska Civil Liberties Union v. State of Alaska, 122 P.3d 781 (Alaska 2005), held affording benefits to spouses of state and municipal employees but not to same-sex partners of employees violates article 1 § 1 of the Alaska constitution, which guarantees "equal rights, opportunities, and protection under the law."

Citizens for Equal Protection v. Bruning, 455 F.3d 859 (8th Cir. 2006), rejects the suggestion on Casebook p. 810 that a state constitutional amendment barring same-sex marriage would violate the Equal Protection Clause of the 14th Amendment. The court distinguished Romer v. Evans on the ground that the state constitutional amendment challenged in that case served no legitimate state interest but the Nebraska amendment barring same-sex unions served the purpose of encouraging "heterosexual couples to bear and raise children in committed marriage relationships." This was sufficient to uphold the Nebraska amendment under the proper equal protection standard, which is this instance is rational-basis review, rather than a heightened level of judicial scrutiny.

The appeal in *Rosengarten* was dismissed as moot because of appellant's death. The Connecticut legislature subsequently passed legislation authorizing same-sex civil unions (Conn. Stat. Ann. § 46b–38bb) and granting partners in civil unions "the same benefits, protections and responsibilities under law . . . as are granted to spouses in a marriage" (id. § 46b–38nn).

Lewis v. Harris, 908 A.2d 196 (N.J. 2006), held 4–3 that although same-sex marriage is not a right under the New Jersey Constitution, same-sex couples must be afforded the same rights and benefits enjoyed by spouses. The court ordered that the state legislature, within 180 days, pass legislation giving same-sex couples such rights and benefits. The dissenters stated that the state Constitution did afford the right to same-sex marriage. On December 14, 2006, the New Jersey legislature enacted a law extending to same-sex couples all the rights, privileges, and duties of married couples, but did not confer the title of "marriage" on the newly authorized civil unions.

A provision of the California Family Code provides for registration of domestic partners and states: "Registered domestic partners shall have the same rights . . . and shall be subject to the same . . . duties under law . . . as are granted to and imposed upon spouses." Cal. Family Code § 297.5. The validity of California's domestic partnership law was upheld against a challenge that it violated California's DOMA-like prohibition against same-sex marriage. Knight v. Superior Court, 128 Cal.App.4th 14, 26 Cal.Rptr.3d 687, 698 (Cal.App. 2005), pet. for review denied, 26 Cal.Rptr.3d 687.

The growing division between states as to how they treat same-sex unions is now beginning to produce interesting conflicts cases. In Alons v. Iowa District Court, 698 N.W.2d 858 (Iowa 2005), the Iowa Supreme Court refused to disturb a lower court decision terminating the civil union of a couple that had entered into the union in Massachusetts. The lower court used its equitable powers to terminate the relationship even though Iowa does not recognize such unions. The Iowa Supreme Court decided that none of the intervenors (mostly church groups) had standing to contest the order. Similarly, in Salucco v. Alldredge, 17 Mass.L.Rep. 498 (Mass.Sup. 2004), the court relied on its "general equity jurisdiction" to dissolve a Vermont *civil union* after Massachusetts had made same-sex *marriage* possible.

In Langan v. St. Vincent's Hosp. of N.Y., 802 N.Y.S.2d 476 (App. Div. 2005), a New York intermediate appellate court reversed a trial court opinion that had allowed to proceed a wrongful death suit brought by a plaintiff whose partner in a Vermont civil union had been killed, allegedly by defendant's negligence. The New

York statute allowed such an action to be brought by a "spouse" and the trial court construed the statute to encompass the plaintiff. The court reversed the trial court and dismissed the action reasoning "the theories of Full Faith and Credit and comity have no application to the present fact pattern." Id. at 479. The dissenting opinion agreed with the majority that neither conflicts nor full-faith-and-credit principles required recognition of the civil union but would have struck down the New York statute limiting recovery to spouses as violating the Equal Protection clause by discriminating against same-sex couples.

May same-sex couples adopt a child and, if so, will the adoption be recognized elsewhere? Close to half of the states permit the same-sex partner to adopt the biological child of the other. See, e.g. In re Jacob, 660 N.E.2d 397 (N.Y. 1995). California goes further: see K.M. v. E.G., infra. Some, like Florida do not: its denial of adoption by a "homosexual" person was upheld against constitutional challenge. Lofton et al. v. Secretary of Dep't of Children and Family Services, 358 F.3d 804, reh. denied, 377 F.3d 1275 (11th Cir. 2004), cert. denied, 543 U.S. 1081, 125 S.Ct. 869 (2005). In contrast, when Virginia children were adopted in another state by same-sex parents, the Virginia court, reversing the court below, ruled in favor of the plaintiffs who sought to compel, by mandamus, the issuance of a new birth certificate. The Virginia statute refers to "adoptive parents" and "intended parents," not to mother and father. The case before the court "is not about homosexual marriage, nor . . . about same-sex relationships, nor adoption policy in Virginia." It is about the issuance of birth certificates only. Davenport et al. v. Little–Bowser et al., 611 S.E.2d 366, 369 (Va.2005). Compare this decision with the functional approach of the court in In re Dalip Singh Bir's Estate, infra Casebook p. 818.

Interstate (or international) recognition may be a different matter still when a claim arising out of a same-sex relationship has been reduced to judgment in F–1. Consider the following two cases. In K.M. v. E.G., 117 P.3d 673 (Cal.2005), the California Supreme Court held (in construing California's version of the Uniform Parentage Act, specifically Cal. Fam. Code § 7613(b)) that, when twins were born after one woman provided an egg for in vitro fertilization and implantation in her partner, both women were the twins' "mothers" and that the parental rights of each continued even after their domestic partnership ended. What about litigation or relitigation of custody or visitation rights in F–2? In the companion case of Elisa B. v. Superior Court et al., 37 Cal.4th 108, 117 P.3d 660 (2005), the court addressed continuing parental obligations: "[A] woman who agreed to raise children with her lesbian partner, supported her partner's artificial insemination using an anonymous donor, and received the resulting children into her home and held them out as her own, is the children's parent under the Uniform Parentage Act and has an obligation to support them." Id. Will another state recognize, enforce, or, when there is jurisdiction to do so, modify the support obligation? See Mariga v. Flint, 822 N.E.2d 620 (Ind.App. 2005): biological mother could sue adoptive mother after the relationship ended. See also infra note 8.

For foreign practice, see infra Casebook p. 811, Note 8. For a survey of the issues addressed above, see Hay, Recognition of Same–Sex Legal Relationships in the United States, in: John C. Reitz & David S. Clark, American Law in the Twenty–First Century: U.S. National Reports to the XVIIth International Congress of Comparative Law, 54 Am.J.Comp.L. 257 (Supp. 2006).

Page 811, Note 8, add:

On July 20, 2005, legislation took effect in Canada legalizing same-sex marriages. Bill C–38, An Act Respecting Certain Aspects of Legal Capacity for Marriage for Civil Purposes (2005). On December 1, 2005, the Constitutional Court of South Africa ruled that defining marriage to exclude same-sex couples was inconsistent with the constitution and invalid. Fourie v. Minister of Home Affairs, Case no. 232/2003 ¶ 49 (S.A. Const. Ct. 2005). The court gave Parliament one year to effect the necessary changes in the Marriage Act and stated that if Parliament did not correct the "defects" within that time, the word "spouse" would automatically be read into the section of the Act now limiting marriage to unions of "husband" and "wife." Just before the expiration of the Court's deadline, Parliament passed, and the Executive signed into law, the Civil Unions Act, Act 17 of 2006 (Nov. 30, 2006). It does not (yet) amend the Marriage Act but provides that partners to same-sex unions shall have exactly the same rights and obligations as persons married under the latter. The act permits religious and civil officers to refuse to marry same-sex couples on moral grounds. Same-sex marriages are also legal in the Netherlands (Wet wan 21 December 2000, Stb. 2001 nr. 9 (Neth)), Spain (on June 30, 2005, the Spanish Parliament passed legislation legalizing same-sex marriages), and Belgium (Code Civil (Feb. 13, 2003) (Belg.), Moniteur Belge, Feb. 28, 2001, at 9880–82). On December 5, 2005, legislation took effect in Britain giving same-sex couples the same social security, tax, pension, and inheritance rights as married couples.

Although same-sex marriages cannot be performed in Israel, the Israeli Supreme Court has recognized same-sex marriages validly entered into abroad in Yosi Ben Ari v. Ministry of the Interior, Case 05–3045 (Consolidated Cases 05–3045, 3046, 10218, 110468, 10597 (Nov. 21, 2006) (Canadian marriage)).

Consider the following information in connection with the second paragraph:

Problems of inter-country recognition have now been important for some time in European countries, many of which recognize same-sex unions in some form, but differ as to the precise legal form (partnership, civil union with marriage-like rights and obligations, marriage). See preceding paragraph, this Supplement.

German law furnishes one example of how to deal with such unions. (German law is summarized in the main text.) Contrary to much European conflicts law (including German) concerning marriage, capacity to enter into a same-sex union is not determined by the home law (law of nationality) of the parties, but—under German conflicts law—by the state maintaining the official (state) register establishing the relationship. Thus, should Swedish, Dutch, or whatever law facilitate conclusion of a relationship that, say, the X-law of nationality of the parties does not, Germany will determine the union's validity and effects (*but see* below) by the "registry state's law." See Coester, in: Münchener Kommentar zum BGB, Vol. 10–Internationales Privatrecht § 17b, anno. 26 (4th ed. 2006). The same law applies to the grounds for the dissolution of a formalized same-sex relationship. Id., at anno. 38. Procedures for dissolution differ from bilateral party agreements (subsequently officially registered), in Denmark, Iceland, Netherlands, Norway, and even unilateral declarations in Belgium, Catalonia, and France, to divorce-like court proceedings in Germany. Id. at anno. 37 n. 79.—What about recognition of unions formalized abroad and their incidents? German law provides for general recognition of foreign unions, but only up to the limit of incidents accorded equivalent unions under German law: § 17(b)(4) EGBGB (Conflicts Statute). For severe criticism of the rule, see Coester, supra, at anno. 88. This "cap" (by German law standards) on the effects of the foreign union in the forum is alleviated by the rule that transactions (litigational or other official issues) finally concluded abroad are to be recognized by the forum. Example, given by Coester, supra at anno. 90: if parties to a Swedish civil union (or equivalent), registered there, adopted a child (not one of theirs) there, the adoption will be recognized as valid in Germany, even though German law would not have permitted such an adoption in the first place. The example also shows that "public policy," an exception to the application of foreign law or the acceptance of foreign official acts or judgments as in all legal systems, does not rise to the level of barring recognition of the Swedish adoption.

More recently, the question has been raised whether recognition of same-sex unions may be required as a matter of European Community law, particularly Directive 2004/38 which guarantees the free movement of EU citizens and their family members. If an EU citizen is married to a non-EU citizen, the latter is a "spouse" and entitled to the same rights of movement and residence as if s/he were a EU citizen himself/herself. Do these rights extend to a same-sex spouse who is regarded as a spouse in the EU country of celebration? A lower German administrative court said "no" in a decision issued before the Directive was adopted. VG Karlsruhe, Decision of Sept. 9, 2004, [2006] IPRax 284. The court's position has now been drawn into question. See E. Jayme, in [2006] IPRax 67, 68. For detailed discussion see D. Coester–Waltjen, Die Anerkennung im Internationalen Personen-, Familien-und Erbrecht und das Europäische Kollisionsrecht, [2006] IPRax 392, 395–96.

How would/should these issues be resolved in the United States—interstate or international?

SECTION 2. DIVORCE

B. EXTRATERRITORIAL RECOGNITION

Page 834, insert in Note:

Von Schack v. Von Schack, 893 A.2d 1004 (Me. 2006), held that a Maine court may, consistently with Shaffer v. Heitner, grant a divorce to a Maine domiciliary without having personal jurisdiction over the other spouse, but may not determine collateral issues of property division, parental rights, or support. The court declined to base its holding on the ground that the action was in rem over the marriage status:

> Because Maine has a unique interest in assuring that its citizens are not compelled to remain in such personal relationships against their wills and because no personal or real property interests would be determined in the proceeding, we conclude that Maine courts have jurisdiction to enter a divorce judgment without personal jurisdiction over the defendant.... We do not, however, alter or re-evaluate the requirement of personal jurisdiction in any other type of litigation affecting the parties' children, financial responsibilities, or property.

> We also caution that when Maine lacks personal jurisdiction over a defendant in a divorce proceeding, Maine courts must exercise their limited jurisdiction

with care. Courts must uphold the due process requirements of notice and an opportunity to be heard and must consider a defendant's assertions of forum non conveniens if the exercise of jurisdiction would further a fraud or create an unwarranted burden or inconvenience for the defendant.

Id. at 1011.

Page 839, add a new third paragraph to Note 4:

The EC Regulation applies only to jurisdiction to grant a divorce to EU nationals or residents. It does not provide a substantive divorce law. The national court with jurisdiction under the Regulation therefore determines the applicable substantive law according to its own conflict-of-laws rules. German conflicts law (as do many other systems) looks to the law of nationality of each of the spouses (cumulatively); a national law that forbids divorce is displaced by German law only when one of the spouses is German. See Art. 17 EGBGB. In a case involving two Syrians, belonging to different Christian denominations, the German court found that Syrian law referred to the applicable religious law and that the latter was Roman Catholic canon law (the *Codex Canonum Ecclesarium Orientalium*). Canon 853 provides that the bonds of matrimony cannot be dissolved by human authority. The divorce petition was denied. The Court of Appeal affirmed, rejection petitioner's arguments invoking German public policy, freedom of religion (she stated that she had ceased being as Catholic), and other claimed constitutional rights. OLG Karlsruhe, Decision of April 23, 2004, 5 UF 205/03, [2006] IPrax 181, with critical anno. by Rauscher, *id.* at 140.

SECTION 6. ADOPTION

Page 869, insert in Note 1:

In February 2006 the U.S. Department of State announced publication in the U.S. Federal Register of final rules on accreditation of adoption agencies and other matters required to enable U.S. ratification of the Convention on Protection of Children and Co-operation in Respect of Inter-country Adoption.

SECTION 7. CUSTODY OF CHILDREN

Page 886, insert in second paragraph:

The Eleventh Circuit stated its strong disagreement with *Croll* in Furnes v. Reeves, 362 F.3d 702 (11th Cir. 2004), rehearing en banc denied 107 Fed.Appx. 186 (2004), cert. denied, 543 U.S. 978, 125 S.Ct. 478 (2004): "... courts in the United Kingdom, Australia, South Africa, and Israel have adopted a broad view of 'rights of custody' and ordered return under the Hague Convention where a child is removed in violation of ne exeat rights. Those courts have stressed the need for enforcement of custody orders (including ne exeat clauses), the spirit of the Convention, and the desirability of uniformity in ordering the return of children removed in violation of a ne exeat provision." 362 F.3d at 717. "Our conclusion today diverges from those of the Second, Fourth, and Ninth Circuits. The seminal United States Circuit Court case is Croll v. Croll.... The Fourth and Ninth Circuits essentially adopted the *Croll* majority's reasoning, as did the district court in this case. ... We, however, join the powerful *Croll* dissent in disagreeing with the majority." 362 F.3d at 719. See case note in 98 Am.J. Int'l L. 851 (2004). See also Silberman, Brigitte M. Bodenheimer Memorial Lecture: Interpreting the Hague Abduction Convention—In Search of a Global Jurisprudence, 38 U.C. Davis L. Rev. 1049 (2005).

Page 886, insert in Note 5 (top paragraph):

The Convention does not define "habitual residence." In a case of first impression, the Second Circuit adopted the following test: the trial court should first determine the shared intent of those responsible to establish the child's residence at the last time they shared such an intent. The court should then inquire whether the evidence unequivocally points to the conclusion that the child has acclimatized to the new location and thus acquired a habitual residence there, notwithstanding the last shared intent of the parents. Gitter v. Gitter, 396 F.3d 124 (2d Cir. 2005). See also Thompson v. Brown, 2007 WL 54100 at *43 (N.D. Ill.). But see Kijowska v. Haines, 463 F.3d 583, 587 (7th Cir. 2006): the *Gitter* test is not workable when the parents have lived apart for a considerable length of time, thus making reference to their "last shared intent" not very helpful. In such circumstances, only the second part of the *Gitter* test helps, representing the case-by-case determination of the child's circumstances which generally already characterizes the case law on this issue

SECTION 8. SUPPORT

B. RECIPROCAL SUPPORT LEGISLATION

Page 897, add at the end of the third full paragraph:

In re the Marriage of Crosby and Grooms, 116 Cal.App.4th 201, 10 Cal.Rptr.3d 146 (2004), the parties had entered into a marital settlement as part of their 1996 Idaho divorce, stipulating the application of Idaho law to their agreement. The ex-wife and the couple's minor children then moved to Oregon, the ex-husband to California, where the Idaho support order was registered. Modification of support was sought in 2001, which the trial court granted, applying the support guidelines of California law. On appeal, held: affirmed. Under California's version of UIFSA, California now had jurisdiction to modify the support order and the application of California law was proper under UIFSA. As to the settlement agreement's choice-of-law clause, the court wrote: "... [D]ue to the special nature of child support, parents are bound by public policy extrinsic to their own agreements. ... [citing cases]. In the present case, since the ... clause requiring application of Idaho law would serve to limit [the father's] child support obligation and undermine the mandate of UIFSA, it is contrary to public policy and is not enforceable. ... Idaho also has passed the UIFSA.... Consequently, Idaho law requires that the guidelines of the forum tribunal—here California be used to modify a child support order. ..." 116 Cal.App.4th at 210.

CHAPTER 13

AGENCY, PARTNERSHIPS AND CORPORATIONS

SECTION 3. CORPORATIONS

C. THE LAW GOVERNING CORPORATE ACTIVITIES

Page 985, insert as new third and fourth paragraphs in Note 4:

The *seat* principle, in those countries adhering to it, applied both to foreign companies moving their seat *into* the country and to local (domestic) companies moving their seat *abroad*. See preceding paragraph, this note. The case law of the EC Court of Justice, supra, makes it clear that the free-movement-of-establishment law of the EU requires recognition of companies validly established where incorporated in the EU. The case law does not affect national law as it deals with its own companies. Might continued application of the seat principle still result in loss of legal personality when such a company moves its seat abroad? A German appellate decision distinguishes strictly between movement into Germany and movement of local companies abroad and suggests that the answer to the question posed is "yes." Bayrisches Oberlandesgericht, Decision of Feb. 11, 2004 (3Z BR 175/03), in: [2004] IPRax No. 4, p. XI. For discussion of European national company conflicts law after *Inspire Art*, see, e.g., Schnelle, Die Regeln des deutschen internationalen Gesellschaftsrechts in der Zusammenschau der Inspire–Art–Rechtsprechung des EuGH und der europäischen und deutschen Gesetzgebung, in: Rasmussen–Bonne, Freer, Lüke, Weitnauer (eds.), Balancing of Interests—Festschrift für Peter Hay 343 (2005); Schurig, Das deutsch-amerikanische Gesellschaftsrecht im Fahrwasser des europäischen?, id. at 369.

While mergers within a member state are possible, cross-border mergers (as distinguished from the acquisition of minority or controlling stock interests) have not been possible, the seat problem being one obstacle. Regulation (EC) 21257/2001, [2001] Official Journal L 294/1, on the Statute of a European Company (SE) provides a vehicle to achieve such a goal. The regulation provides for the establishment, by one of more companies, of a *Societas Europea* (SE) which is free to move its center of operations within the Community. It is a *European*, rather than a national company, although regulatory or protective provisions of national law (such as worker codetermination under German law) may carry over into the way such a company may need to be structured. As the first company to avail itself of this new corporate form, the German insurance and banking giant Allianz AG decided in early 2006 to transform itself into Allianz SE and, as part of that process, to acquire the Italian insurer Riunione Adriatica di Sicurtà Spa. The merger documentation can be found at www.allianz.com/azcom/dp/cda/0,,353413–49,00.html.

Page 997, insert as a new third paragraph (fourth paragraph of Note 1):

Compare VantagePoint Venture Partners v. Examen, Inc., 871 A.2d 1108 (Del. 2005), summarized supra this Supplement in connection with Casebook p. 360 (Delaware adheres to law-of-incorporation rule), with Friese v. Superior Court, 36 Cal.Rptr.3d 558 (Cal.App. 2005): internal-affairs rule does not preclude suit against corporate officers and directors for insider trading under California law because that law does not regulate, but rather protects, the corporation and its shareholders and because California had sufficient contact to apply its law. Does the Friese court's distinction between regulation and protection answer the question raised in the first paragraph supra? Did the decision in *CTS* turn on the sufficiency of Indiana contacts?

*

Documentary Appendix:
Conflicts Law in the European Union

Page 1071, add the following Notes at the end of No. 5 on the Enforcement Order Regulation:

NOTES

1. The Enforcement Order Regulation was adopted and is now in force in the European Community (except Denmark). [2004] Official Journal L 143/15. As stated in the text, the Order applies to "uncontested claims," as defined above. In the main, these will be judgments entered by default. Thus, if a debtor wishes to avoid application of the Enforcement Order Regulation, he or she needs to appear and contest the claim. This circumstance has the effect of possibly broadening the jurisdictional reach of the rendering court, "submission" becoming a practical necessity for the defendant: see Geimer, Internationales Prozessrecht anno. 3182 (5th ed. 2005).

2. If the defendant does contest the claim in the first state, the Regulation does not apply. If the defendant lost in the first state, enforcement must then be sought under the enforcement provisions of the "Brussels–I" Regulation (supra at p. 1015 et seq.). The judgment debtor will then have available the defenses provided by that Regulation's Art. 34 et. seq. (supra Casebook p. 1014). Note that, in contrast to the Brussels Convention (which Brussels–I replaced) and to the Lugano Convention, defenses to the first court's judgment are no longer considered ex officio by the recognizing court, but only upon the debtor's motion and then only upon appeal and not at the trial level. Brussels–I, Arts. 41, 43, 45, supra Casebook pp. 1015–16. Consider the defenses available under Brussels–I: does the defendant, who stayed out of the first state, really gain much by now having defenses at the enforcement stage?

3. If the defendant did not contest the claim in the first state, the Regulation applies and, as the text notes, the ensuing "European Enforcement Order" can be executed directly in the second state, without the need for a formal exequatur order under local law. Looked at from a traditional, public international law perspective of state sovereignty, this extraterritorial reach of the first state's enforcement power is "almost revolutionary." Geimer, supra, at anno. 3178; see also Geimer, in [2002] IPRax 69, 71. Rather than using the mechanism of the European Enforcement Order, the judgment creditor is still free to use the enforcement procedures of Brussels–I, supra.

4. National civil procedure law provides defenses against the enforcement and execution of judgments. Under German law, for instance, a judgment debtor may move ("bring an action") against execution of a judgment (Vollstreckungsabwehrklage) under § 767(2) ZPO (Code of Civil Procedure) on defenses that have arisen after the conclusion of (final) oral argument in the original action. For examples of such post-rendition court decisions, see Zöller–Herget, ZPO Kommentar, § 767 anno. 12 (24th ed. 2004). One of these might be assignment by the judgment creditor of his judgment to another. This remedy is not regarded as permitting a review of the rendering court's judgment on the merits, but to provide a remedy for post-judgment occurrences. To what extent should these national remedies continue to be available when enforcement is sought under a European Order (especially if such remedies differ among the member states)? Should relief have to be sought in the original court or would doing so enlarge its jurisdiction beyond that contemplated by European law (supra note 1, at the end)? Review interstate enforcement in the United States.

Page 1071, add a new subsection 6 (before Part II):

6) Legal Aid for Cross–Border Disputes

The Regulations set out and commented above at pp. 1002 and 1028 (jurisdiction in civil and commercial matters and in matrimonial matters, as well as execution of judgments resulting therefrom), presuppose access to the courts of another Member State to sue in the first place or to enforce a judgment. Costs may prevent some claimants to do so. Cost may also prevent defendants to answer suit in another Member State. An EC Directive (see a few excerpts below) addresses this problem. A "directive," under European law is a binding command to the Member State(s) addressed to bring about the legislative goal specified, but leaving the means of implementation to each State. The following directive was addressed to all Members (except Denmark, which has opted out of this type of legislation).

Council Directive 2002/8/EC to Improve Access to Justice in Cross–Border Disputes by Establishing Minimum Common Rules Relating to Legal Aid for such Disputes

[2003] Official Journal L 26/41

Article 1

. . .

2.   [The Directive] shall apply, in cross border disputes, to civil and commercial matters whatever the nature of the tribunal. . . .

Article 3
Right to Legal Aid

1.   Natural persons in a dispute covered by this Directive shall be entitled to receive appropriate legal aid in order to ensure their effective access to justice . . .

2.   Legal aid is considered to be appropriate when it guarantees:

(a) pre-litigation advice with a view to reaching a settlement . . . ;

(b) legal representation in court . . . ;

In Member States in which a losing party is liable for the costs of the opposing party, if the recipient loses the case, the legal aid shall cover the costs of the opposing party, if it would have covered such costs had the recipient been . . . habitually resident in the Member State in which the court is sitting. . . .

Article 4
Non-discrimination

Member States shall grant legal aid without discrimination to Union citizens and third-country nationals residing lawfully in a Member State.

Article 5
Conditions Relating to Financial Resources

1. Member States shall grant legal aid to persons ... who are partly or totally unable to meet the costs of proceedings....

[Member state authorities assess financial ability according to general criteria provided in para. 2.]

Article 7
[Related Costs Covered by Second State]

[In addition to the costs referred to in Art. 3(2), the second state covers costs of translation and interpreters' services.] [The state of domicile—Art. 8—covers preparatory costs incurred in that country.]

Article 9
Continuity of Legal Aid

1. Legal aid shall continue ... to cover expenses ... in having a judgment enforced in the Member State where the court is sitting.

2. A recipient who in the Member State is sitting has received legal aid shall receive legal aid provided for by the law of the Member State where recognition and enforcement is sought.

3. Legal aid shall continue ... if an appeal is brought either against or by the recipient....

...

Article 12 et seq.
Procedure

[Omitted]

Page 1072, delete top three full paragraphs and replace with:

In 2003, the Commission issued a Green Paper on the possible conversion of the Rome Convention into a Rome–I Regulation (see COM(2002)654(final)) as well as a proposal for a Rome–II Regulation to deal with non-contractual obligations (see COM(2002)0427(final)). Both projects have since undergone many, in some respects significant changes. As of this writing, two proposed regulations are in various stages of the legislative enactment process. For the proposed Rome–I Regulation, see the Commission Proposal (COM(2005)(final)) and the opinion of the Economic and Social Committee (2006. O.J. C 318/10). For the proposed Rome–II Regulation, see: Commission Proposal (COM(2006)83(final)), Common Position Adopted by the Council (2006 O.J. C/289E/04), and Parliament, Recommendation for a Second Reading of Dec. 22, 2006–A6–0481/2006 (final).

The following presents the existing Rome Convention, with Notes that explore some of its provisions and call attention to some of changes that have been proposed for Rome–I. Material on non-contractual obligations and on the proposed Rome–II Regulation concludes the Appendix.

Page 1083, Consumer Contracts, insert at end of first paragraph:

But see change to top paragraph of Casebook p. 1084, infra.

Page 1084, replace top paragraph, beginning with sentence starting in line 5, with:

The proposed Rome–I Regulation would remove this inconsistency; its Art. 5(2), para. 2 (Commission version) would parallel the Brussels–I approach. However, the Commission proposal would introduce new problems. Art. 3(1) provides for freedom of choice of the applicable law by the parties, "without prejudice to Art. 5" and subject (Art. 3(5)) to mandatory rules of Community law. Art. 5(1) provides for the application of the rules of the *Member State* in which the consumer has his or her habitual residence. If a German seller and an American consumer conclude a contract and select the law of a third country, that country's law—and not the more consumer-friendly German or American (non-member state) law will govern in a German court (assuming jurisdiction), absent only a mandatory rule of *Community*, not German national, law that is protective of the American consumer. See Leible, Internationales Vertragsrecht, die Arbeiten an einer Rom I–Verordnung und der Europäische Vertragsgerichtsstand, [2006] IPRax 365, 369–70.

Page 1084, after top paragraph, insert:

Note that, substantively, consumer protection may result from applicable Community law and thus supplement or displace national law. See particularly, Niglia, The "Rules" Dilemma—The Court of Justice and the Regulation of Standard Form Consumer Contracts in Europe, 13 Colum. J. Eur. L. 125 (2006/2007).

Page 1084, *Mandatory Rules*, insert before (1):

Introductory Note: "Mandatory rules" and their effect as overriding a choice-of-law reference or, indeed, making an inquiry into the applicable law irrelevant in the first place, have proved to be a subject of great difficulty in the work on the proposed Rome–I and Rome–II Regulations. When are mandatory rules (of national law) "international" mandatory rules (for instance, in the sense of No. 1, following) and when are they merely "local" (in the sense of No. 2, following)? Is a Community consumer or other protective rule always an "international" mandatory rule (as in No. 1)? What is or should be the effect of another state's mandatory rule (see No. 5, following)? Is there a difference in content or in time of application between a mandatory rule and the rejection of a legal rule on public policy grounds (see No. 4, below)? The resolution of these issues in the proposed Regulations is as yet not clear.

Page 1085:

Ireland and Portugal have also opted out of 7(1).

Page 1086, top line—delete sentence starting on that line and replace with:

The material below reproduces the 2003 Commission Proposal and provides comments to it. Since that time, the Parliament has commented and the Commission and Council have reacted with revised proposals. For the latest proposed Regulation version, see Draft Regulation of the European Parliament and the Council on the Law Applicable to Non–Contractual Obligations (Rome II), Official Journal C 289E. 28/11/2006, p. 68. It is widely expected that a Regulation will be adopted and promulgated in 2007 (probably to enter into effect within 6–12 months thereafter), there will be changes and adjustments between now and then. We therefore do *not* include the current proposal at this time, but retain the 2003 version, with only occasional references to the current proposals (see also the additions, supra this Supplement, to pp. 516 and 533). For summaries (in German) of the current draft, see Wagner, Internationales Deliktsrecht, die Arbeiten an der Rom–II Verordnung und der Europäische Deliktsgerichtsstand, [2006] IPrax 372; Hay, Internationales Privat-und Zivilverfahrensrecht No. 139 (3rd ed. 2007).

Page 1100, insert a new No. 6a):

Section 2 (Arts. 9 et seq.) of the text reproduced above applies to "non-contractual obligations arising out of an act other than a tort or delict." In Continental law these are obligations sounding in unjust enrichment (Art. 9(3)) and claims based on having performed an act for another without having been authorized to do so ("*negotiorum gestio*," often translated as "agency without mandate") (Art. 9(4)). For discussion, see D. Sheehan, *Negotiorum Gestio*: A Civil Law Concept in the Common Law?, 55 Int'l & Comp. L. Q. 253 (2006). The Commission's current draft proposal for a Rome–II Regulation assigns separate provisions to these two obligations. Art. 10 essentially reflects the prior Art. 9(3). In contrast, Art. 10 on negotiorum gestion differs from Art. 9(4). It calls for the application, in order, of the law applicable to a previous relationship between the parties, the law of the parties' common habitual residence, or the place of acting, all of the foregoing subject to the application of a more closely connected law. Note how this formulation tracks the provisions of the general tort article (Art. 3 in the earlier draft, reproduced at Casebook pp. 1088–89). For the, quite parallel, rules of the new Japanese conflicts statute, see supra, this Supplement, changes to Casebook pp. 518–19.

Page 1101, Note 8), add at the end:

See also, supra this Supplement, addition to Casebook p. 1084 (Introductory Note to *Mandatory Rules*).

Page 1102, add to Note 11:

For an American perspective, see Weintraub, Rome II and the Tension Between Predictability and Flexibility, in: Rasmussen–Bonne, Freer, Lüke, Weitnauer (eds.), Balancing of Interests–Festschrift für Peter Hay 451 (2005) = 41 Rivista di diritto internazionale private e processuale 561 (2005).

†